Sanctuaries of the Goddess

Goddess and Child,
Vinča Culture,
Drenovac, Yugoslavia

SANCTUARIES *of* THE GODDESS

The Sacred Landscapes and Objects

by Peg Streep

Principal Photography by Cindy A. Pavlinac   Robert Zehring   Michael Reagan   Blaine Harrington III

A Bulfinch Press Book   *Little, Brown and Company*   *Boston   New York   Toronto   London*

First Edition

"Myth" by Muriel Rukeyser from *Out of Silence,*
1992, TriQuarterly Books, Evanston, Illinois,
© William L. Rukeyser.

Library of Congress Cataloging-in-Publication Data
Streep, Peg.
     Sanctuaries of the Goddess : the sacred
     landscapes and objects of the Goddess /
     Peg Streep. — 1st ed.
                      p.   cm.
     "A Bulfinch Press book."
     Includes bibliographical references and index.
          ISBN 0-8212-1976-6 (pbk.)
     1. Goddesses — Europe.   2. Sacred space —
     Europe.   3. Goddesses — Middle East.
     4. Sacred space — Middle East.   5. Europe —
     Antiquities.   6. Middle East — Antiquities.
     I. Title.
              BL473.5.S76   1994
291.3'5'0901 — dc20   93-10342

Bulfinch Press is an imprint and trademark of Little,
Brown and Company (Inc.)
Published simultaneously in Canada by Little, Brown
& Company (Canada) Limited

PRINTED IN SINGAPORE

*For Alexandra, whose being radiates
with the power of the Goddess; and Peter,
who is the other half of myself; and Jane
Lahr and Judith Mitchell, good friends
both, who introduced me to the Goddess*

Contents

Sanctuaries of the Goddess

PRECEDING SPREAD:
**Temple of Athena (Temple
of Ceres), Paestum.**
OPPOSITE: **Standing Stones
of Callanish.**

1 Realms of the Goddess

Sanctuaries of the Goddess is designed as a visual journey of re-creation, an effort to reconnect in the reader's imagination those sacred precincts of the Goddess, landscapes and sites, some fashioned by nature and others by humanity, with the artifacts now stored and displayed behind glass in museums. The scholarship of Gertrude Rachel Levy, Marija Gimbutas, and Vincent Scully, among others, has taught us that the sites (and later the edifices) as well as the creations of the human hand and imagination — the paintings, designs, figurines and sculptures, and pottery — were meant by our ancestors to invoke the Goddess in all of her aspects, her powers, her essences.[1] The terrain covered by this book in text and illustrations encompasses thousands of miles and, of course, many thousands of years, so that even the landscapes reproduced here must be restored, with the aid of the text, by the eye within — so that we may glimpse what once was.

To complete this process of restoration we must counter the progress of civilization. We must imagine the megalithic stones that were reused for farmhouses and dwellings by those who came after returned to their holy sites, and reroute the vehicular traffic that has transformed how people use and see the landscape. An internal restoration needs also to take place: of habits of mind, of seeing and understanding the ancient ways, in order that we may reexperience the real power and awe these sanctuaries actually inspired. The first layer of modernity we need to strip is our own complacent conception of nature. For most of us, living in electrically lit apartments and homes, darkness has meaning only when we are unable to turn a light on or when we find ourselves in unfamiliar circumstances. The moon may remain an object of pleasure, of beauty and romance, but in the modern world it merely hangs above us, separate from how we live. We no longer look toward it to light our way at night, or to its stages to serve as our calendar. The cycles of the seasons, the rising and setting of the sun, only secondarily mark time for us: we no longer feel that they immediately affect our survival. Lightning, thunder, and other once potent natural phenomena have been stripped of their portents and symbolism; when we are trapped in an open field during a storm, our knowledge of how lightning works defuses its formerly terrifying power. Only the most devastating of natural catastrophes — earthquakes, severe floods, volcanic eruptions, for example — retain their primal effect and meanings. But long before Zeus wielded the thunderbolt or Poseidon managed the oceans or the God of the Old Testament created Heaven and Earth, the power of the Goddess was the power of nature in both its life-giving and death-wielding aspects. Indeed, as Vincent Scully has suggested, certain sites prone to earthquakes, such as Knossos, may

Autumn Dawn over Crete, Sacred Island of the Goddess

The Sacred Spiral

Spirals appear on the walls of Paleolithic caves, symbolizing, as Marija Gimbutas has explained, the sacred energy or life force of the Goddess. They are associated for millennia with other sacred symbols, particularly the horn and the snake. Spirals were used to depict the Goddess and to invoke her appearance in many cultures, on artifact and edifice alike, on temples in Malta and on tombs in Brittany and Ireland. This example is from New Grange in Ireland, where it figured in midwinter rites of renewal. (For more, see page 113.)

have been deliberately chosen as sacred to the Goddess precisely because they embodied her danger.[2]

Lost to us too, in many respects, is a sense of the mystery of nature and of the cycles of life — that intimation of larger patterns that imbued the Goddess with awe and reverence. Scientific knowledge tends to supplant our adult sense of mystery with understanding: this is how a seed germinates, how a tree flowers and bears fruit, how an embryo is created. Although it may take an event of truly momentous import, such as the birth of a child or a near escape from death, to reconnect us to the mysterious, the rites and rituals, the sacred precincts, and even the artifacts of the Goddess resonate with it. The nature of the Goddess is neither the "Nature" glorified by the nineteenth-century Romantic poets nor the pastel-colored landscape filled with anthropomorphic creatures by Beatrix Potter; its mysteries are profound, its bounties inseparable from its dangers and violence.

Our intellectual habits separate us from the Goddess as well. We have been brought up to recognize and categorize things as either A or B; to divide time into past, present, and future; to see, as Marija Gimbutas has noted, life and death as opposites, not part of a continuity; to experience "life" as here and the "hereafter" as somewhere other, physically elsewhere.[3] (This last legacy, articulated by Plato, runs through Christianity, linking the Elysian Fields with Heaven. The promise of eternal life is located skyward, where the sky god reigns.) There is ample evidence that the sacredness of the Goddess and her sites lies not in "either/or" but in the awesomeness of *and:* life *and* death, beneficent *and* punishing, fecund *and* arid, eternal *and* finite. Rediscovery of the ways of the Goddess requires that we compensate for the intellectual distance between the ancient times and our own, that we see in the womb-shaped tombs of Sardinia, for example, not simply a metaphor of regeneration but, rather, belief in rebirth itself.

Historically and spiritually we are distanced from the Goddess by the succeeding patriarchal societies and their religions, which began with the incursions of the pre–Indo-Europeans in the fifth millennium, who brought with them a religion of sky gods, an entirely different religious symbolism and ethos. What resulted from this initial clash was a hybridization of values, with those of the patriarchy in dominance. The succeeding millennia furnished our culture with layers of patriarchal myth and iconography, which need to be stripped away so that we can reclaim the past.

The sacred landscapes and sanctuaries of the Goddess speak to us not only in different terms but in a different language, one that is both visual and spiritual. The language of the Goddess is symbolic, as has been brilliantly exposed for us by the pioneering work of Marija Gimbutas, and is reinforced by the evident and persistent power of these symbols from the Paleolithic era through ancient Greece and, perhaps, in folklore

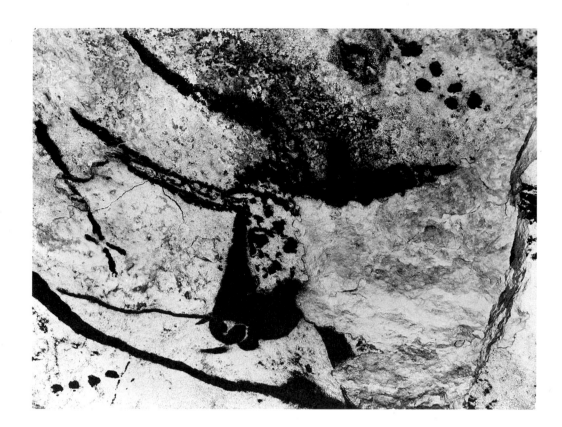

**Bull from the Cave
at Lascaux**

The cave as a holy place
began in the Paleolithic, and
it continued to be seen as
holy through Roman times.
Deep in the Goddess' body,
the earth, humanity wor-
shipped and made offerings.
The bull and its horns
proved an enduring symbol
of regenerative energy and
spiritual power. Painted
and engraved on the earliest
caves, perhaps as an invocation to the Goddess to assure
the plenitude of the herds,
the bull and its horns would
be part of the sacral setting
of the Goddess at sites as far
apart in distance and time as
Çatal Hüyük, Sardinia, and
Crete. While in Indo-European culture and myth the
bull is a masculine symbol,
in the culture of Old Europe
it is firmly associated with
the Goddess and renewal.

and language even up to modern times. We see it in the trail of red ocher that colors the
dead with the hue of life, from the caves of the Dordogne in 30,000 B.C. to the burial sites
beneath the sleeping platforms of the living in Çatal Hüyük twelve millennia later. Three
thousand years later, ocher still covers the dead at the great necropolis, the Hal Saflieni
Hypogeum in Malta. Red ocher and other pigments color the Goddess too in her life-
giving aspects: the pregnant, red-stained Venus of Laussel; figurines stained red from the
Cucuteni culture; the red painted bulls' horns of Sardinia. The expressionless, white
Cycladic statues were buried along with the bones of the dead in red ocher, while in
classical Greece the blood-red pomegranates of Demeter at Eleusis remind us again that
red is the color of life. We relearn the meaning of continuity when we realize that to enter
the great inner chambers of the Upper Paleolithic cave, men and women crawled on their
stomachs through dangerous passageways and waters in darkness, with the cave's ceiling
only inches above their heads, and then sometimes dropped down many feet through
narrow shafts, a ritual as well as literal journey that clearly imitated the physical aspects
of being born and its dangers. Twenty-five thousand years later, in the fourth century B.C.,
that earlier process repeats itself in more formalized ways, but in the same ancient forms,

15

as the Mysteries of Eleusis. The continuity of symbols forces us to realize that our most cherished notion, that the advancement of civilization necessarily entails complication and the laying aside of old ways, is not necessarily true. The Goddess, as we shall see, continues to appear in her more "primitive" forms — for instance, as an unadorned stalagmite emerging from the depths of a cave; as an uncarved pebble — long after she also has achieved realism in her features and modeling. Much of what we define as *civilized* (and its opposite, *barbaric)* we have, of course, learned from the classical Greeks, and, as the last chapter in this book will show, their trouble with the Goddess was no accident.

It is important, too, to remember that symbolism does not necessarily imply abstraction, distance, or loss of emotional power. The stalagmite representing the Goddess in her earthbound aspects continues to be worshipped in many different cultures *contemporaneously* with fully rendered statues and figurines. By the same token, the landscape symbols of the Goddess, whether caves or rock shelters or the horns and breasts that Vincent Scully has located in Minoan and Greek sites, are not merely naive personifications familiar to us both from folklore and Romantic poetry (that is, the shape of a sleeping giant in the profile of a mountain range) but are potent and moving evidence of the Goddess' presence. The idea that certain places and locations are inherently sacred, as representatives of a larger divine force, is very old indeed, first evident to us in the clear distinctions between caves as shelters or habitations and caves as sacred sites.

While *Sanctuaries of the Goddess* chronicles the ultimate suppression of the Goddess and the triumph of the male sky gods in all their various forms, it also testifies to the tenacity of the ancient power of the Goddess. This tenacity is defined by the twenty-five thousand years during which the Goddess occupied the center of human life, and by the reflection of the old ways in the civilization of the new: in Homer and in the art, literature, philosophy, and architecture of classical Greece. We see it too in the concerted efforts of the advocates and proponents of patriarchal religions to remove any trace of the Goddess. The difficulty of displacing the Goddess is preserved not only in the written record, including the Old Testament and the injunctions of the early Christian fathers, but in the enduring, if unwritten, record of folklore and traditions. It is reflected, too, in the incorporation, both conscious and unconscious, of the old ways of worshipping the Goddess in the new religions.

Some of this tenacity reflects what the Goddess offered humanity (and the sky gods did not); some of it doubtless rests in the power of tradition and the comfort of old ways. But some of the holding power of the ancient practices lies, I believe, precisely in the tradition of the sacred landscape: a shrine required no walls, no edifice, no mark of identification. A hillock, a cave, a rock shelter sufficed. Since the Goddess' presence is

Holy Cistern at the Palace of Zakros, Minoan Crete

In the advanced civilization of Minoan Crete, the presence of lustral basins, located near shrines in the palaces, attests to rites connected to water, perhaps involving purification of celebrants. At Zakros, fragments of ceremonial vessels and offerings were found in ritual areas where water seeped up from the earth, including both the Spring Chamber and the Well of the Fountain.

The Tomb of New Grange, Ireland, on the River Boyne

The sacrality of water in the religion of the Goddess also begins in the Paleolithic, when both sacred caves and rock shelters were located near or above water. Water as divine moisture remained part of the sites sacred to the Goddess, connected to her roles as life-giver and as chthonic power, from holy caves in Italy to shrines in Crete and tombs in Ireland. Streams and rivers themselves might well have been considered holy in the religion of the Goddess, as the concentration of tombs and barrows around the river Boyne in Ireland suggests. The evidence of specific rituals and ritual vessels pertaining to water underscores water as holy, as does the development of a consistent iconography in the culture of Old Europe—net motifs, striations, meanders, and, later, ships of regeneration —associated with the life-giving nature of water.

imaged in the natural landscape, a stalagmite indicates her being as surely as does the handiwork of humanity. We need to remember, too, how intimately our ancestors knew the landscape in which they lived out their lives and on which they depended, how familiar it was to them, and how they noted its seasonal and cyclical changes, the dying off of the old and the birth and growth of the new. The sacred landscape has implications in reconstructing the ways of the Goddess, as it did for the leaders of the new patriarchal religions. The later traditions of the sacred building, whether Judaic, Christian, or Islamic, temple, cathedral, or mosque, enclose a sacred space and pose a firm distinction between the sacred space within and the profane space without. (In fact, the enclosed space was considered so separate from the geopolitical entity, the land or country on which it stood, that it became traditionally a place of asylum.) The shrines of the Goddess located in the landscape consistently deny the separation of the sacred and profane; even the buildings that enclose the votaries in the shape of the Goddess' body, such as those on Malta, are a continuation of the earth on which they stand. In Crete, for example, sacrifice of the sacred animals would be accomplished both within and without the palaces; there is evidence as well that certain rites were performed within at an altar, but that others were performed in a stand of trees, an equally potent symbol of the Goddess.[4] For the patriarchal religions, the existence of the sacred landscape meant that simply forbidding graven images was of no avail. The building of Greek temples and then churches in many of these precincts is eloquent testimony to the power of the old ideas, as is the sight of an ancient menhir in France transformed by carving into a Christian monument.

There is, undeniably, a great deal that separates us from many of the peoples discussed in *Sanctuaries of the Goddess*, but one thing has *not* changed in the course of some thirty thousand years: humanity's struggle with the facts of life and death, the reality of death and the hope of renewal. Human beings first mastered fire, then animals by hunting, and then gathered and initiated the growth of the seeds of the earth to survive. Yet their triumph remained tempered by their understanding of their part in, and their belonging to, the greater, larger cycles of earthly life. Thus their dead or their bones were laid to rest within the earth, so that they might begin again where they started: in the body of the Goddess from whom all life and death emanated.

We should begin to look for the Goddess where Clement of Alexandria, some seventeen hundred years ago, exhorted his fellow Christians *not* to go:

"Do not there seek diligently after godless sanctuaries nor after mouths of caverns full of jugglery. . . . As for the old stump honored by the desert sands, and the oracular shrine there gone to decay with the oak itself, abandon them both to the region of legends now grown old."[5]

Iconography of the Goddess: Carving from Locmariaquer, Brittany
(3500–3000 B.C.)

Once dismissed as mere decoration, the signs and symbols of humanity's spiritual expression from the Paleolithic to the Neolithic have begun to be deciphered by scholars. Although precise interpretation is still a subject of discussion, the existence of a sacred iconography as early as the Paleolithic has been demonstrated by the work of Annette Leming, André Leroi-Gourhan, and others; those of the Neolithic, with a wide range of examples from various cultures, have yielded to the patient scrutiny of Marija Gimbutas and other scholars.

Brittany, in France, has roughly a thousand megalithic tombs, some of which bear the most detailed carved examples of the symbolism of the Goddess. On an endstone of a chamber tomb at Locmariaquer, a symmetrical arrangement of opposed crooks or hooks in four rows has an oval at its center. The hook appears on other stones, as well as anthropomorphic stelae and menhirs. Marija Gimbutas identifies the oval as a vulva and thus asserts that the stone represents the Goddess herself, with the hook acting as a simplified single spiral or symbol of divine energy.

Goddess Stele ("La Dame de St. Sernin"), Rodez, France (Third Millennium)

As the source of all, the Goddess presides over death, often in the form of an owl, a bird that through the millennia separating us from the Neolithic maintained its association with death in folklore and tradition. Throughout Western Europe, the Owl Goddess is depicted in many forms, ranging from the schematized — showing eyes and eyebrows only — to the more fully articulated, with beak, necklaces, and breasts on stele and menhirs. Even in her aspect of death, though, the Owl Goddess also holds forth the promise of regeneration. According to Marija Gimbutas, the symbols associated with the Owl Goddess — triangle, zigzag, net, and vulva, among others — are those of regenerative power.

Even when the Goddess is superseded by the pantheon of the sky god Zeus, her attributes are passed on to Greek goddesses, and it is the warlike Athena who inherits her owl, reminder of her ancient predecessor's chthonic power.

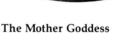

Minoan Snake Goddess

Unlike the serpent of
Indo-European and later
mythology, the snake was a
symbol of life-giving energy
from the Upper Paleolithic
through the culture of Old
Europe and Minoan civilization. The snake's coiling
movement made it a symbol
of energy, while its ability
to shed its skin made it a
powerful symbol of regeneration. Being of the earth,
the snake was also a symbol
of the Goddess' chthonic
power. The sacred energy of
the snake is expressed as
well in the abstract symbol
of the spiral.

The Mother Goddess

The Goddess is also the
Mother of all, as this image
of the Goddess with child
tells us. In the cultures of
Old Europe, the Goddess
as "protectress of young life,"
in Marija Gimbutas' phrase,
was depicted variously in
human, bird, snake, or bear
form. From the Mavro Spelio
cemetery near Knossos on
post-palatial Crete (c. 1350
B.C.) comes another vision of
the Goddess as the "Great
Mother," as Erich Neumann
called her, this time lifting
the child in a gesture of celebration. Rendered in terra-
cotta, her shape identifies her
as the Earth Mother as well.

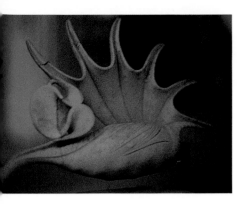

**Minoan Clay Seashell
from Phaistos** (2000–1700 B.C.)

The ancient belief that water
was the source of life associated the Goddess as creatrix
with the waters; the shell,
from the Paleolithic onward,
is a potent sacral symbol,
associated with life-giving
powers. Shells were, for millennia, buried with the dead.
On Minoan Crete, seashells
paved the floors of shrines,
and as exemplified by an
engraved gem from the sacred
Idaean Cave, which depicts
a woman blowing a triton
before an altar crowned with
the horns of consecration and
a bough, shells were used
to invoke the Goddess. Shell
forms on Minoan Crete were
imitated in alabaster and in
clay. Even in the pantheon of
the sky god Zeus, the goddess Aphrodite was born out
of the foam of the sea, and
is often depicted on a shell.

Author's note: Throughout this book, I have used the word *Goddess* to denote the life-giving and death-wielding female deity who figures in rite and ritual from the time of the late Paleolithic and Neolithic eras through what Gimbutas has termed "Old Europe," who figures even later on the islands of the Aegean and in the Mediterranean, and whose reflected presence still animates certain of the rites, sacred artifacts, and architecture of classical Greece. Even though I have used the term throughout, preferring it to any of the alternatives, I do not mean to imply, for example, that the Goddess as worshipped at Çatal Hüyük was identical to the Goddess venerated on Malta, even though there is clear evidence not only of their similarities but also of the tantalizing possibility that they are connected. So too the iconography of the Goddess in Ireland and in Brittany hints at a real connection, although one that remains, for the moment at least, unprovable. The ground-breaking scholarship and research of the last thirty years has rightly striven to elucidate the hidden symbolic vocabularies of ancient societies, focusing, as they needed to, on the similarities and continuities. The symbolic character of the archaeological evidence has required interpretation, and the work of interpretation has long been helped by a Jungian approach that again tends to emphasize similarities, not only among ancient cultures long since vanished but also among the folklore and rites of more recent societies.

Aristotle supposed that human nature is everywhere the same and that fire burns here as it does in Persia. So does the Jungian approach, perhaps best exemplified in the work of Erich Neumann and, more popularly, Joseph Campbell. Yet equally fascinating is the individual stamp of belief and creation articulated in the different societies that worshipped the Goddess — an imprimatur echoed in the varying visions of the Goddess and the delineation of her sacred sites. I have tried to use both approaches in this book, a venue open to me since I have the luxury and privilege of drawing on the research of great writers and scholars.

A note on chronology: there are two ways of establishing the dating of archaeological artifacts. The older method, radiocarbon dating, was used in many of the sources written before 1990 that are cited in the Selected Bibliography. The newer method, dendrochro-nology, which recalibrates radiocarbon dating, is used consistently by archaeologist Marija Gimbutas in her works. These dates are consistently earlier (that is, the artifacts are older). I have used dates determined by dendrochronology, drawn from sources, for the reader's ease in using this book in conjunction with the most up-to-date works of reference.

2 *The Sacred Cave*

The moss, lit and floating in fat, held in small, hollowed-out lamps of stone, must have cast a smoldering light upon the jagged walls. In many places, what flickering light they had with them could not have penetrated the darkness; in the recesses, outlines and flashes of color hovered in and out of view as their eyes adjusted to the darkness within, deciphering shape and mass in the cave's depths. Women and men listened with ears pricked for the sounds of animals who used the caves as well, their labored breathing magnified by the echo of the cavernous depths. Traversing the caves was not easy: bent backs, bellies scraped by crawling, limbs bruised and flesh rubbed raw by rock, footholds lost. At Lascaux they dropped into the dark, over twenty-six feet down, holding on to a rope. Elsewhere, they groped in the dark, hanging on to the stalactites, fording subterranean rivers, the force of the waters below them loud in their ears. At Les Trois Frères they walked first through subterranean corridors of rock, then crawled through a pipelike tunnel and negotiated a rock chimney, one foot on either side of a chasm. It was only then that they reached the center chamber. Bodies against the hard rock, labyrinthine paths, vertical drops: at Labastide the descent is a vertical pit, and the cave yields, one hundred feet down, into a second pit with only a narrow ledge to gain entry into the sacred chamber. La Pasiega in Spain is entered by way of a manhole, below which roars a subterranean river; here, the most dangerous precipices are painted with signs and animals.[1]

Hidden within these natural labyrinths scattered throughout the hill country of southwest and southern France and northern Spain, to be rediscovered only in the twentieth century, are amazing expressions of humanity's yearning spirit, symbols and representations that speak across the distance of some twenty-four thousand years. Impressions of the human hand, traced with charcoal or color or perhaps blown onto the walls; meanders; triangles, symbol of female fertility; other geometric figures. Animals inhabit the darkness, their forms painted high on the ceilings and deep in the recesses. Like the caves themselves, the representations they contain are remote and inaccessible, in places not chosen for ease. Close to smooth, spacious wall spaces that could have been easily painted, humans chose inside recesses instead, requiring the painters to be "crouched sideways or lying on their backs or completely doubled up, scarcely able to spare, from supporting their own weight, a hand to steady the feeble lamp, still less to trace the bold, firm shapes of their vision."[2] These secret spaces were also hard for participants in the rites of the cave to see, set as they were in high places requiring a dangerous climb or on a ceiling shrouded in darkness; at La Loja, six oxen are engraved "on the summit of a pyramid of stalagmite, where the face and body of the beholder are pressed against the

The Rotunda, Lascaux

decorated surface."[3] While the Great Hall of the Bulls (the Rotunda) at Lascaux, a space roughly fifty-five feet long and twenty-two feet wide, could (and perhaps did) accommodate a hundred people gathered within its walls,[4] elsewhere the Lascaux Cave narrows almost to impassability. The Meander becomes one foot four inches wide, yet figures were painted here, in a space so small that photographs cannot be taken of the art.[5] The Meander ends as an impenetrable tunnel, marked in red by a sickle-shaped sign and a dot. The art in the caves of the late Paleolithic era rarely appears near the cave's entrance as it does earlier in human history: the depth of the inner chambers and their difficulty of access seem to have held increasingly specific ritual and sacral meaning. The superimposition of cave art, engraving upon engraving, painting upon painting, while the adjacent wall is bare, suggests too, in Fernand Windel's words, "a deliberate pursuit of the mysterious and secret; in fact, a ritual intention."[6]

The awe-inspiring art of the late Paleolithic caves is itself an outgrowth of an even earlier religious tradition, one connected to the earth and feminine sacrality. Contemporary with the earliest cave sanctuaries are female statuettes, some with exaggerated curves, others that are sleek stylized visions. While they are collectively referred to as "goddesses," they nonetheless seem to represent specific types or visions of the universal force that animates the life cycle. The breasts and belly of the Willendorf Goddess, found in Austria and dating from 30,000 to 25,000 B.C., intimates pregnancy and maternity; the deep triangle incised between her legs is femaleness in its totality. Carved of limestone, her body still bears traces of the sacred red ocher; tiny (about four inches high) but nonetheless retaining the volume and weightiness of the stone out of which she is carved, she is a personal, not communal, religious artifact — she fits in the hand. A second figurine found at Willendorf reminds us of the varied vision: this one is carved out of ivory, considerably larger in height (ten inches), and sleek in proportions. The exaggerated curves and mass of the Lespugue Goddess, from circa 23,000 B.C., deny her scale: carved out of mammoth ivory, she is not even six inches high. She was found in a hearth in a shallow cave overlooking a gorge. And although, like the Willendorf, she embodies fecundity, it is in a very different form: the deliberate egg-shaped stylization of her breasts and buttocks make it clear that she is a symbolic artifact embodying a sacred concept. Marija Gimbutas has suggested that she is a vision of "intensified fertility," that the repeating egg shapes of her body are the "power of two."[7] The egg shapes so dominate her shape that they create a visually meaningful confusion: she both bears them and is them. The pubic triangle is echoed by triangles on the back of her buttocks, as well as a triangle of ten incised lines on her back; Anne Baring and Jules Cashford connect these lines to the waters of birth as well as to the ten lunar months of pregnancy.[8]

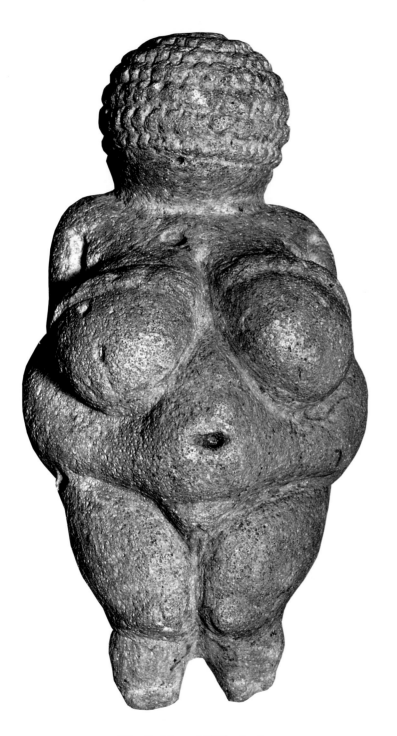

The Goddess of Willendorf

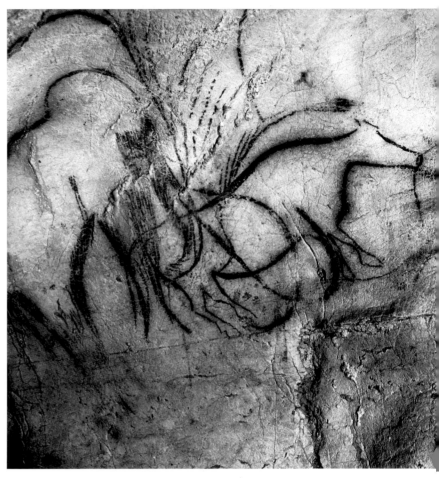

Detail of Wall Art from Pech-Merle Cave, France

Pech-Merle is a labyrinth of underground passages that extend over a mile and a quarter. A mammoth, a cow, and incomplete outlines of other animals are shown in this detail. In addition to wall art and stalactites naturally formed in the shape of breasts, this cave complex contains a ceiling covered with literally hundreds of macaronilike marks scraped into the once soft clay as part of ritual.

LEFT: **The Grimaldi Goddess**

Found near Menton on France's Côte d'Azur, right on the border of France and Italy, this statuette of the Goddess was one of ten found in a series of caves and shelters first excavated in the 1870s. Her curves — particularly those of her buttocks — are so exaggerated as to render them clearly symbolic.

CENTER: **The Lespugue Goddess**

RIGHT: **The Goddess of Sireuil**

Found at the entrance to a small cave in the Dordogne, this figurine is carved out of hard calcite. Marija Gimbutas has identified the pronounced buttocks of the Goddess as she is realized in the Paleolithic and, later, as symbolic of a creation myth involving a cosmic egg laid by a bird.

Other statuettes are images of nurturance reduced to its stylized essence. From Dolni Vestonice in Czechoslovakia come an ivory pendant of breasts and an ivory rod with breasts, incised all over with lines (both circa 24,000 B.C.). Divine nurturance is expressed in an entirely different way in another Goddess from Dolni Vestonice, found in the ashes of a hearth. Made of clay and ground bone, she is slightly under five inches tall. She is faceless; her eyes are indicated by slits, from which emanate lines that stream down her pendulous breasts, hanging low on her belly. On her, the sexual organs are absent; she is instead an emblem of the "divine moisture" emanating from the Goddess' eyes.[9]

But the female deity of the Paleolithic era is the source of *all*, both life and death, and it is this second aspect we most see in the figures from the Péchialet and Laugerie Basse caves in France, and from Malt'a in Siberia: these are stiff figures, their arms lifeless, with clearly marked pubic triangles. They are light- or bone-colored, what Marija Gimbutas has called "the color of death."[10] This Goddess presides over the end of life, and while she begins in the Paleolithic, she will find her fullest expression later in the white figures of the Neolithic Cyclades.

All these Paleolithic Goddesses are archetypes of a female force, commanding both life and death. That they are also sacred figures in the Paleolithic context, even though most of them were found in domestic settings, is underscored by engravings at the earliest cave sanctuaries which predate the Goddess figurines, notably the deep vulvae carved into the walls of caves in the Dordogne in France at Abri Cellier, Castanet, and La Ferrassie. These remind us simply and powerfully that, in Gertrude Levy's words, the cave itself had long been "a Mother."[11] Clearly the interiors and spaces of the sacred caves recall the vaginal canal and womb of the female body; that the process of entering the cavernous womb of the earth entailed dangers directly analogous to, not merely symbolic of, the dangers of birth hints at the extraordinary emotional power of these early religious rites.

The caves themselves and, within them, the locations for symbolic representations and figures of animals were chosen precisely because they were already considered to be sanctified places, distinct from the caves and shelters that served as places of habitation. For we must remember, as Mircea Eliade tells us, that even these early caves and the carved and incised figures of the Goddess are not themselves really the beginning. Artifact and site are the beginning only because they are where our evidence begins.[12] They do not necessarily reflect the beginnings of humanity's religious spirit, or even of the beginning of the worship of a female deity. We have evidence that prior to 30,000 B.C., human beings buried their dead, believing in some survival after death, and sprinkled the bones with red ocher or hematite, the color of blood, the fluid of life, as humans would for thousands of years to come. As N. K. Sandars has noted, "Belief in life after death, and in the efficacy of a visual sign" had very early on become part of humanity's growing complexity.[13] At the cave of La Ferrassie in the Dordogne, Neanderthal people buried the body of a child under a stone slab, the underside decorated with pecked-out cupmarks in pairs. The belief in the "efficacy of a visual sign" is crucial to the religion of the Goddess, for this belief gives rise in time, in the absence of written language, to a long-established sacred iconography that revealed and invoked the Goddess for thousands of years. The cupmark, like ocher, would remain a consistent symbol of both the presence of the Goddess and her powers of regeneration throughout the Neolithic era and in places separated by both distance and time. At La Ferrassie, too, a ditch had been dug near the human burials, containing animal bones and cinders — offerings perhaps to the dead or to the Goddess of the earth who held the dead in her depths.

In the absence of artifacts with a symbolism decipherable to modern eyes, which may not, after all, mean that they are void of meaning, Eliade has suggested that the tools of humanity which predate the Aurignacian era (30,000 B.C.) must have been "charged with a certain sacrality." Humanity's first technological discoveries — "the transformation of stone into instruments for attack and defense, the mastery over fire" — gave human beings the gift and means of survival and "produced a universe of mythic-religious values and inspired and fed the creative imagination."[14] We see hints of this older, now unrecoverable inspiration still embodied and at work in the spirituality of the Paleolithic, where we start, since the force of spiritual tradition is strong indeed. By the Upper Paleolithic, when the bodies of the dead were coated in ocher, shells and ivory and bone ornaments were deposited in the graves. E. O. James suggests that in addition to the ocherous symbolic blood, shells, cowries among them, accompanied the dead precisely because they resemble the shape of the female labia, and thus figured in a "life-giving rite" for the dead, a birth after death.[15] Like the cupmark, the shell would not only be part of the burial of the dead for millennia, it also would serve, in Minoan Crete and elsewhere, to invoke the Goddess. Through the figures of the Goddess and the sacred precincts, caves and rock shelters, we can begin to rediscover the human beings who inhabited the European continent between 30,000 B.C. and the start of the Neolithic era twenty thousand years later and, perhaps, recover their spirituality.

The dense concentration of painted and decorated caves in the Dordogne of France hints that the area itself was once a spiritual center as well as, in George Bataille's words, "a focal point of a civilization."[16] It seems probable that the Valley of the Vézère was the place where the huge herds of reindeer crossed, migrating to the pasturelands of the Auvergne. Here the hunters waited for the herds each year, assuring themselves and their people of a plentiful food supply; in a harsh world, this was a place of plenty. The earliest of the decorated cave sanctuaries, from approximately 30,000 to 27,000 B.C., had their holy places located close to the mouth of the cave, where the engravings, scratched onto blocks of stones and pebbles with a flint burin, would have received daylight. It was only later that depth appears to have become a part of religious ritual and that art and symbol, first engravings and then paintings, moved deeper into the earth. At the cave of Pair-Non-Pair, about twenty yards deep, the decorated surfaces were illuminated by daylight. At La Grèze, they were in shadow but clearly visible. At La Mouthe, a cave used over an extensive period of time, only the later art was found in the deep interior. (This progression appears, according to Leroi-Gourhan, to be true of the Spanish caves as well: at Los Hornos, the first and earliest sacred chamber was lit by daylight. At a later period, that chamber was abandoned for others that formed a natural labyrinth seventy-five yards deeper into the cave.[17]) From this same period are the vulvae incised at Castanet, Abri Cellier, and La Ferrassie, as well as the outlines of parts of animals preserved in the stone: forequarters at La Ferrassie and heads at Abri Cellier.

The Gargas Cave, spacious and easily accessible, is about 150 yards long and its width varies from 22 to 44 yards; daylight not only reaches the back of its first chamber but also illuminates the turn to the second. At Gargas, some 150 negative impressions of hands appear on the walls, either stenciled or blown on in red, yellow, and black. The hand motif occurs at later caves as well, including Pech-Merle and Les Combarelles. On the clay film of the walls at Gargas are meanders, drawn with the fingers. The hand and the meander would continue as important parts of the sacred iconography of the Goddess through the Neolithic, both alone and in combination with other symbols. Marija Gimbutas, working back from Neolithic examples, particularly those at Çatal Hüyük, has identified the hand as symbolizing the "energizing touch of the Goddess" and the meander as a symbol of water.[18] Max Raphael reminds us that the hand was the enabling organ that permitted humanity's "spiritual and physical forces to strive forward," and that secured both safety and food. He posits an important relationship: "If the world was conceived after the image of the hand, it was conceived as an abundance of forces, and these physical and magical forces must conversely find their representation in the hand."[19]

The identification of the meander with water as a life-giving source specifically connected to the earth is borne out by the location of shelter sanctuaries near or above water. The Roc aux Sorciers near Angles-sur-l'Anglin (Vienne, France) was a 160-foot ledge above a stream with a small cave at one end. Here were carved three life-size female figures, the portions of the body below the waist worked in low relief, with an emphasized pubic triangle. Like the figurines of the Goddess whose facial features are anonymous and whose limbs taper off into nothingness, the heads and even upper bodies of these female figures appear never to have been worked. Traces of paint signify that these figures might once have emerged visually and powerfully from the rock on which they are carved. Life-size ibexes as well as smaller horses and bison were also carved at this shelter.

At Laussel, two contiguous rock shelters, one 450 feet and the other 65 feet long, are separated by a gully overlooking the Beune River, and surmounted by a spring. The reliefs found here, as well as other artifacts, indicate that this was a sacred place. The most beautiful of these reliefs is, without question, the Goddess of Laussel, which may be as old as 25,000 B.C. Carved on a limestone slab, she measures seventeen inches in height; traces of red ocher still color her head and body, suggesting that once she was the color of the blood of life. Her breasts hang heavily. In her raised right hand she holds the horn of a bison, while her left hand, resting against her rounded, perhaps pregnant belly, draws our eyes to her vulva. On the bison horn are thirteen notches, perhaps indicating the lunar months. The horn she holds was itself already possessed of a complex symbolism. Neanderthal men at La Chapelle-aux-Saints buried the tusks of a mammoth, while at Brno *Homo sapiens* buried tusks in a bed of ocher; it seems likely too that hunters would have associated the growth of horns and antlers of animals with breeding cycles as well as power. Does the Goddess of Laussel hold the power of the moon in her hand, the cycles that marked the fertility of the animals, the annual return of the herds, or is the notched horn a symbol of procreative power, as it would be thousands of years later in Crete?[20] Or does the layering of symbols hint at "not a single identity, but many connected identities: the huntress, guardian of the animals, guardian of fire, midwife, mother, lover"?[21]

The other surviving engravings at Laussel intimate that the rituals of humanity were indeed, by 25,000 B.C., already possessed of symbolic complexity. Two other Goddesses adorned the walls of the shelter. One also bears traces of ocher, and although the relief is not as finely carved as that of the Goddess with the horn, she too has pendulous breasts, exaggerated buttocks, and a pronounced pubic triangle. Because of damage to the relief, we can no longer identify the object held in the left hand. Her head is stylized, her hair divided into quadrants, while her right hand rests by the side of her body. A third Goddess once existed in the shelter but was destroyed during World War II. From castings, we know that she too was largely faceless, with pronounced breasts, buttocks, and pubic triangle. She held her right hand out straight from her body; in it was a rounded object, interpreted by some as an animal stomach or bladder to hold liquid.[22] Were these images of the Goddess part of a sequence, each of them endowed with a different sacred object? Two other Laussel reliefs, alas, give us no clear answer. One of them is usually identified as a male, perhaps a hunter, because of the lean body, the pose, and the absence of female sexual characteristics. As Henri Delporte has pointed out, however, the figure may not

The Goddess of Laussel

actually be male, since he connects the form to those figures from Laugerie Basse and Péchialet, which Gimbutas has identified as the Goddess in her aspect of death.[23] The last relief, that of a double-headed figure, is like those mirror images of royalty on playing cards, and it has been variously interpreted as an image of copulation, of birth, or simply a superimposition of two entirely separate engravings.[24]

What rites may we imagine taking place at Laussel, surrounded by water above and below? Phalluses, whole and in fragments, were found in the strata, as were circles of stone inscribed with vulvae, and figures of animals, including a female deer. Were these rites of regeneration and birth, celebrating the return of the herds or the eternal cycle? Were they rituals of thanks and offerings to representations of the earth, taking place within a shelter of the earth? Or did they celebrate the waning and waxing of the moon in the sky and the parallel cycle below, the womb of the earth and those of the earthly females coming forth to give birth?[25] Can we conjecture, as Alexander Marshack has, that the symbolic objects in the shelter are evidence of a combined myth, with the Goddess as a central character, the forerunner of the great Goddess of the Neolithic?[26] We cannot know precisely, of course, and yet the consistent symbolism of the site must surely speak to the great themes of birth and regeneration: the ocher, the breast and belly, vulva and phallus, the horn and the moon. Gertrude Levy has suggested that the facedown position of the reliefs when they were found was not the handiwork of later generations or intruders out of touch with the old rituals but part of the original rites: images of the Goddess, like the cupmarks of the Neanderthals, faced the earth in order to invoke her.[27] We have evidence that the open-air, rock shelter site of Laussel, as well as others, continued to be used even when the places of ritual began to move deeper into the body of the earth. This seems to hint at the possibility of two different rites, perhaps serving different needs and uses, the one performed in the daylight or half-light and shadow of the shelters, the other in the dark interior of the cave. While N. K. Sandars stresses the contrast between the open-air sites and the caves, and the art contained in them — the one "accessible, almost domestic" and the other "secret, inaccessible, remote from the mundane world"[28] — as testifying to rituals of the everyday and those of the supernatural, the existence of both seems as well to articulate a complex spirituality that may have also encompassed a mythology that was far from "primitive" and endowed with considerable texture and complexity.

The voices that animated the rites of the sacred cave have long been silenced; the only testimony left to us is that of the caves themselves and the art left upon their walls. It may well be that some of the natural characteristics of the caves initially suggested their sacrality: the "feminine" characteristics of certain caves, such as the oval niche at Font-de-Gaume, the fissure at Niaux, or the breastlike forms of stalactites at Le Combel, at Pech-

Merle, may have enhanced their ritual meaning. The "masculine" connotations of the Shaft at Lascaux may have underscored the cave's basic symbolism as the fertile womb of the earth. In the same way, as art historians have noted, the ability of the artist to integrate certain natural rises and formations on the caves' walls into both painting and relief may have increased the sacrality of the iconography and image by incorporating the contours of the sacred earth into artifact.[29] And while it is difficult to imagine certain caves or parts of them being used on a frequent, communal basis because of inaccessibility or danger — the hundreds of bears' dens that were found at Rouffignac, for example — others clearly might have been.

The cave of Lascaux is essentially one long corridor, 110 yards long from end to end, off of which runs an axial passage and a shaft. With the exception of the Shaft, the cave is accessible; indeed, its scale and that of its paintings seem to suggest not only large gatherings of people but also organized ritual. The natural layout of Lascaux is a progression from one discrete and defined chamber or area to another, indicating that there may have been a close relationship between the shape of the cave and the rites themselves. As at the cave of Les Trois Frères, there is evidence that the precincts of Lascaux were visited frequently, although we cannot know whether these visits were months or years apart, centuries apart, or, for that matter, millennia apart. The great Rotunda, a U-shaped cavern with a nineteen-foot ceiling, would have enclosed the assembly once it entered the cave, perhaps led by a shaman or priest. Above the people's heads, flickering in and out of shadows, the remarkable frieze of black and red animals might have seemed to move as the gathering moved through the natural hall. Painted against the white of the cave walls, the five great bovine figures, some of them over seventeen feet long, two of them facing a row of three, must have seemed possessed of supernatural size and energy. Iconographic signs — strokes, dots, a barbed symbol — may have annotated the figures for the participants, endowing the images with even greater sacrality.

If the procession continued into the Axial Gallery, the ceiling above their heads would have lowered some seven feet, and they would have found themselves at a keyhole entrance to a winding, twenty-yard-long corridor that narrowed and widened by turns; in places, there is barely enough room for two people to pass each other. Here, the figures of gigantic bovines and stags would have emerged from the darkness, along with horses surrounded by barbed signs as well as a huge bull with a barbed sign in front of its nose. Farther along, a procession of horses, once again with a barbed symbol, decorates the wall; the last horse appears to be falling backward into a recess. While traditionally the barbed symbols have been interpreted as animals, more recently Leroi-Gourhan identified them as female symbols, while Alexander Marshack has suggested instead that they

represent stylized plants and trees, symbols of the earth's fruition.[30] Both of these interpretations rightly raise the symbolism to a higher plane than that of primitive hunting "magic," and although the precise lexicon of this ancient iconography has been lost to us, it is clear that they drew attention to, and perhaps annotated, the sacral meaning of the images on the walls. We must finally agree with Riane Eisler that "along with the first awareness of self in relation to other humans, animals, and the rest of nature must have come the awareness of the awesome mystery — and practical importance — of the fact that life emerges from the body of a woman."[31] The rites of the caves and the shelters were inextricably bound up with that awareness. The Axial Gallery narrows and becomes a constricted tunnel, ultimately impenetrable; its dead end is marked with red. The movement of the rites from an open rounded space to one progressively more constricted mimics birth, the inner contours of the female body, and the sexual act.

The other route off the Rotunda leads to the Passageway, the least well preserved part of the cave and perhaps the oldest. While it is long (fifty-five feet) and wide (ten to thirteen feet), its ceiling ranges only from three to five feet high: here the participants in

LEFT: **Detail from the Frieze of the Rotunda (Hall of the Bulls), Lascaux**

The auroch at the right side is eighteen feet long and more than eleven feet above the modern level of the cave's floor. The floor level would have been even lower in prehistoric times, suggesting that scaffolding must have been used to paint the figure. To the left of the auroch's head is a dagger-shaped sign. Below the red cows are red signs, which Mario Ruspoli suggests may be plant stems.

Lascaux Cave

Detail of a painted frieze of a fabulous beast and wild horses. The beast is over five and a half feet long.

rites must have had to crawl at least part of the way. The Passageway is full of engravings, made with flint burins, as well as paintings. Beyond the Nave, the corridor narrows to the Chamber of Felines; this chamber, approximately thirty feet long, is unique among the caves for its paintings of felines. It contains thirty animal figures and a great many signs; it too ends with red markings. Off the Nave lies the Apse, which in turn leads to the Shaft. A small round chamber with a fifteen-foot diameter, the Apse is covered with thousands of engraved lines, superimposed over engravings and paintings of oxen, stags, and horses. While some of the superimpositions are decipherable as animals, others are ritual symbols such as parallel lines, barbed figures, ovals, and "comets." The presence of these engravings in close proximity to the Shaft suggests a place of ritual ceremony, what Mario Ruspoli has called the cave's "most sacred place."[32] Here, the body of the earth was first inscribed with sacred markings by the participants, who then descended through the Shaft into the very womb of the cave, more than twenty feet below. We know that they lowered themselves down the Shaft by rope: opposite a small ledge on one wall, which would have afforded a precarious foothold, is an elaborate painted panel showing a wounded, disemboweled bison, a long spear, a retreating rhinoceros who defecates as he leaves, and a crudely drawn felled man with an erect phallus, wearing a bird mask. His hands, too, are birdlike. Two bird-head objects, as well as barbed signs, are also shown; what may be the bowels of the bison or a representation of the vulva spill out in concentric ovals. A profusion of lamps and spears found in the rubble at the bottom of the Shaft suggests that, despite its inaccessibility, it was visited frequently.

The precise meaning of this numinous panel eludes us; among the readings that have been suggested, all of which assume that it is indeed a narrative, are a hunting anecdote, a prostrate shaman, or the flight of the spirit from both the human and the animal bodies.[33] It could as well be a portrayal of a ritual conducted by a shaman.[34] Anne Baring and Jules Cashford suggest that the painting (along with the Sorcerer from the cave of Les Trois Frères) attests to the existence of two central myths, one the myth of the Goddess and the second the myth of the hunter. In their analysis, the Goddess myth was concerned with the eternal order, while the hunter myth spoke to the mundane world of survival; the shaman mediated between these two myths and worlds of experience in the rites of the caves.[35] The mysterious and secret placement of the panel intimates great spiritual importance; the images of death, the presence of the vegetative barbed signs, the erect phallus, and the bird's head (symbol in the Paleolithic and the Neolithic eras of the Goddess of death and regeneration) speak indirectly of rites of regeneration within the earth, and of a myth of considerable complexity. We should, however, heed Alexander Marshack's wise counsel and permit the symbols of the Paleolithic — the pregnant doe at

Lascaux Cave

Two bison, painted back to back, cover eight feet of the cave's wall.

Altamira, the mare at La Pileta, the horse at Les Trois Frères, for example — to be "storied signs" or "open equations," symbols that can be read and used at different levels of story and meaning.

From other caves in France and Spain come other glimpses of sacred iconography and rituals, many of which would become more fully expressed in the religion of the Goddess of the Neolithic era. At Altamira in Spain, meanders and spirals were traced onto the clay walls. In the Neolithic, these symbols gain strength as signs of the Goddess, and reach their apogee in the carvings at New Grange in Ireland, where the triple spiral of the Goddess would be illuminated by the midwinter sun in the house of the dead. At Pech-Merle, female silhouettes with exaggerated buttocks, breasts, and bellies are traced onto a clay-filmed ceiling amid meanders that partly obscure them. The birdlike head of one of these tracings suggests that, like the figurines, she is the precursor of the Bird Goddess of the Neolithic.[36] Also at Pech-Merle, breast-shaped stalactites with nipplelike protrusions were decorated with black and red dots, raising the natural similarity in shape to the level of symbol. While it is not possible to ascertain whether the images of the animals portrayed in the caves functioned as part of a representational or symbolic vision (or both), it is worth noting that many of the animals emerge in the Neolithic as clear epiphanies or aspects of the Goddess. At Les Trois Frères, an engraved lioness with her cubs peers out from the wall; many thousands of years later, on Minoan Crete, lions will flank the Goddess as the Goddess of the Mountains. Are the three snowy owls in the same cave the precursor of the owl of the Neolithic, symbol of the death aspect of the Goddess?[37] At the cave of Niaux, a bull painted on the floor carries within its body three eggs; the egg as symbol was already evident in the carved Goddess of Lespugue and will continue to be a sign of the Goddess of regeneration for millennia to come.

In the Neolithic, the fish becomes associated with the Goddess, particularly with the womb and the process of becoming; at the sacred site of Lepenski Vir, it is the Goddess as fish who is the presiding deity over the rites for the dead. But already, at the Paleolithic cave of Pech-Merle, two back-to-back horses were filled in with black dots and surrounded by negative hands; a red fish is painted inside one horse. An engraved antler from Lorthet in France shows realistically rendered fish springing up between the legs of stags or reindeer; above the head of one of the animals are two lozenges, each punctuated in its center by a slash. Both the Pech-Merle horses and the antler engraving exhibit symbols that will persist in the language of the Neolithic Goddess. The fish will remain the emblem of the womb;[38] the connection between the fish and the womb, as Buffie Johnson has

Altamira Cave (Spain)

Unlike some of the other sacred caves, Altamira is relatively accessible, although its chamber with the painted ceiling, about eighty-five feet from the entrance, must have always been shrouded in darkness. Near the entrance to the cave, a broad area is covered with meanders and figures drawn in the clay with fingertips — perhaps part of the sacred ritual.

noted, is made crystalline by a carved sandstone fish from Malt'a in Siberia, dating from the Paleolithic, for the center of the fish's body bears a pecked-out spiral labyrinthine design in the shape of a womb, with a uterine passage.[39] The hands, symbol of the Goddess' energizing touch, will find their complete expression at Çatal Hüyük in the middle of the seventh millennium, where handprints in black (signifying fertility) and in red (sign of the blood of life) decorate the shrines. The lozenge, probably a schematized icon of the vulva and the pubic triangle, is found on the bellies, buttocks, and breasts of the Cucuteni Pregnant Goddesses in the middle of the fifth millennium.

The shadows of millennia obscure our vision of Paleolithic rites. We may imagine women (for the size of the negative handprints corresponds to the contemporary female skeletons) and men entering both the rock shelters and the sacred caverns. Children too penetrated the depths of the caves; their heel marks pock the floor of the cave of Tuc d'Audoubert, as well as those of Pech-Merle and Niaux. Although some scholars have adduced juvenile rites of initiation from these prints, Leroi-Gourhan argues persuasively that the location of the footprints in areas quite separate from those we imagine to be central to the rites testifies equally to a vision of children playing and running freely.[40] The figure of the so-called Sorcerer at Les Trois Frères, as well as the bird-head man at Lascaux, has also been a subject of conjecture. While the Sorcerer has been positively identified by some scholars as the representation of an actual shaman who led the rites of the cave, the figure may yet be symbolic. Marija Gimbutas suggests alternatively that the bison man associated with the herd at Les Trois Frères may well be a Master of the Animals, a deity who often figures in hunting mythology.[41]

Though the rites of the sacred caves are obscured, nonetheless the symbolism of the Goddess of the hunters manages to shine through the thousands of years that separate us. It is in the next stage of humanity, the shift from hunting to agriculture, that the outlines of the Goddess etched in the Paleolithic will burgeon with full dimension, luminosity, and meaning.

Lascaux

The cave-womb of the earth
holds the image of plenty,
the reindeer.

3 The Roots of Old Europe

The gradual acquisition of the arts of agriculture and the domestication of animals over a period of thousands of years changed the basis of human survival. Also transformed, inevitably and intricately, were humanity's relationships to plants, animals, and, finally, the earth. The mastery of planting and harvesting seed could only have come from a sustained and intimate examination of plants: their parts, their cycles of growth, and the larger patterns of growth, dying off, and renewal in nature.[1] So too the first domestication of feral animals, the dog in some places, the sheep or pig in others, must have begun with intimate observation of each species. The great Goddess of the Neolithic reflects those intensified relationships between human beings, plants, and animals in ways that are both distinct from, yet connected to, the older vision of the Goddess embodied in the Paleolithic.

The complexity of symbolism in the Neolithic underscores not only the religious and spiritual complexity of the Neolithic peoples but also their diversity. The Goddess as she is realized in the various cultures has an underlying cohesion, brilliantly demonstrated by the ground-breaking work of Marija Gimbutas, yet the voices that speak to us through the sites and artifacts articulate collective needs and visions that possess an individual stamp. The shift from hunting and gathering to agriculture, both gradual and erratic because of its evidence in one culture and then absence in a succeeding one, redefined the deity. She now presided over the earth, its wild fruits, and its herds as one who was the provenance of all that promised humanity survival: Goddess of the Grain, Mistress of the Animals, Goddess of the Waters.[2] Human effort aligned itself with and depended upon the company of the Goddess. As the relationship of humanity to the flora and fauna intensified, so did its relationship to the Goddess, without whose help the renewal of the earth and the growth of crops would not take place. The nomadic life of the Paleolithic, when the great herds dictated both where and how women and men would survive, was largely lost. Instead, established communities with more permanent structures of habitation grew, as did the great dependency of human beings on the beneficence of the forces of nature embodied in the Goddess. Along with pests and droughts, another aspect of the natural cycle confronted the earliest farmers: the earth dying beneath them, refusing to yield her fruits. In Italy and elsewhere, the land was cleared of forest by fire, the ashes were pushed back into the soil, and the seed planted. But without crop rotation, fertilization, or plowing, there would come a time, ten years or perhaps thirty, but at least once during a human lifetime, when the clearing would simply yield no more.[3] The new nomadism of the farmers was based on the fruits of the earth and the search for arable land, not the fleet-footedness of the herds. The Goddess of the Neolithic is no mere fertility

Enthroned Goddess, Pazardzik, Bulgaria
(c. 4500 B.C.)

Lozenges and flowing lines are inscribed on this clay Pregnant Goddess: on each buttock a lozenge, symbol of fertility, declares her preeminent role as the Goddess of the fields. (Marija Gimbutas has noted that similiar statues actually have grain pressed into the lozenges.) While her face is masked and her mouth is indicated only by holes, her broad hips make her bound to the earth.

totem to ensure crop renewal but a presiding deity over all of the cycles of life, human, animal, and plant.

As women's and men's relationship with nature and its cycles took on texture and complexity, so too their vision of the sacred landscape moved beyond the cave, while continuing to include it, and became iconographically denser. At Çatal Hüyük in Anatolia, excavations revealed a culture that lasted for roughly one thousand years, from the end of the eighth millennium to the end of the seventh, with twelve layers of habitation. Çatal Hüyük is in many ways the precursor of sacred traditions that would find their apogee in Minoan civilization, and we may speculate that the actual site on the Konya Plain may have been chosen for its position and view of sacred mountains. Çatal Hüyük was a city with houses close together, sharing common walls; the houses were entered with ladders through holes in the roofs. The people who built it were settlers from elsewhere who brought with them seeds for planting in the rich soil of the plain, close to the river, the Çarsamba Çay.[4] Even today, the Konya Plain remains one of the most important agricultural areas in Turkey. Then, the plain teemed with wildlife for hunting, among them aurochs, wild pigs, and red deer. On a clear day, the twin-coned volcano of Hasan Dağ, some eighty miles away, would have been visible from Çatal Hüyük: its eruption is depicted on a painting on the walls of one of the shrines in the city. An active volcano until sometime in the second millennium, Hasan Dağ must have been a potent symbol of the Goddess' force and destructive power as the wielder of death. At the same time, Hasan Dağ was probably also one of the sources of the obsidian on which the prosperous economy of Çatal Hüyük was based, and therefore functioned equally as a symbol of the Goddess' fruits. To paraphrase James Mellaart, the excavator of Çatal Hüyük, obsidian was valued not only for its cutting power, its transparency, its reflective power, and jet black appearance, but also for its symbolism: chthonic in origin, linked to the land of the dead and the Goddess of death, it was nonetheless a "true gift of mother earth and therefore imbued with magical potency."[5] Mirrors of obsidian were buried with the dead in shrines, but are not found in houses.

Did the twin cones of the volcano suggest the breasts of the Goddess, as the modeled breasts that protrude from the shrine walls at Çatal Hüyük symbolize her life-giving power? Or did the cleft between the peaks epitomize the sacred triangle familiar from the Paleolithic? Or did they embody the sacred power of the bulls' horns, so much a part of the religious symbolism of Çatal Hüyük? While there is no precise answer, all these symbols of the sacred landscape echo throughout the painted and modeled shrines of this ancient culture, and were even more clearly expressed on Crete, thousands of years later, where the older tradition of the sacred landscape would be more formally articulated.

Excavation Site, Çatal Hüyük

What remains on the surface leaves no hint of the extraordinary civilization that once flourished here.

More twinned horns, these the rocky and rugged peaks of the Taurus (Bull) Mountains, also formed a part of the sacred landscape of Çatal Hüyük. The river that watered the plain began in these mountains; the trees that supplied the city with wood grew there. The Anatolian leopard, an animal that served as a symbol of the Goddess, roamed them. In addition to worshipping in the shrines contained within the city, the people of the plain visited the caves of the Taurus Mountains. There they collected stalactites, some in natural shapes resembling breasts, udders, and human figures, and brought them back to the shrines in the city. Some of them were partly sculpted while others were used in their natural form, for at Çatal Hüyük aniconic form and realistic representation existed side by side.[6] This ritual custom hearkens back to the Paleolithic but looks forward as well to religious patterns that persist throughout the Neolithic in Malta and Crete. Among the dominant images of the religion of Çatal Hüyük are bull horns, both alone and in conjunction with other symbols, as both painted or modeled representations, as well as real horns incorporated into shrines, and in paintings of bulls. One such figure — a huge, six-foot-long bull painted in red — appears in a shrine surrounded by tiny, insignificant male human figures, and appears to depict a symbolic relationship rather than a hunting scene since, while some of the men are armed, the animal is not wounded. It is painted on the north wall of the shrine, the wall facing the Taurus Mountains, and, as James Mellaart noted, at Çatal Hüyük images of bulls always occupy the same position relative to the mountains in every shrine.[7]

The Goddess as she is realized at Çatal Hüyük presides over the forces of life and death, not as opposing states but as part of a greater continuum; indeed, the burial practices of the community also suggest a continuity between the rites of the living and the bones of the dead, which were buried beneath the sleeping platforms of houses and shrines. The bodies of the dead were probably taken to an open-platform charnel house, perhaps built of wood and reeds, outside of the settlement, where vultures picked the flesh off the bones prior to burial.[8] The terror and awe that this aspect of death inspired in the people of the city is made clear by the paintings on the wall of the Vulture Shrine, where seven vultures, with horrifyingly lifelike wingspans of five feet, feed on the bodies of six small, headless humans. Yet if the Goddess presided over the vultures of death, she also presided over them in conjunction with life: in another shrine, a pair of woman's breasts protruded from the wall. Within each of the molded breasts was the skull of a vulture, and from each red painted nipple a vulture's beak sprang forth, the reality of the life force and that of death compressed into a single visual image of great power. In other shrines, representations of breasts contained the skulls of foxes and weasels. The image may too, according to Marija Gimbutas, represent the "cycle of being 'eaten back' into that primordial source which gives birth and nourishment to all life."[9] The bones of the dead may have been brought within the buildings at either a spring or summer ceremony that coincided with the annual whitewashing of the city's interior walls. James Mellaart has suggested that the shrine burials were the bones of the individuals who were privileged in some way in this Neolithic society; some of the bones, mainly those of females, were drenched in red ocher.[10]

Religion was central to life on the Konya Plain, as demonstrated by the fact that of the 139 rooms excavated at Çatal Hüyük, more than 40 were devoted to religious rite and ritual. Although we have little evidence of the precise nature of the ritual practices, the vision of the deity of Çatal Hüyük is clear. The imagery of birth is pervasive. In a mobiliary statue found in a grain bin, the Goddess is supported by flanking leopards while she gives birth; her location suggests that she was placed in the bin to encourage the continuing fruition of the earth. In another shrine (VIB 10, numbered by the excavator for its level and position), a Goddess with her legs spread and heels upturned is shown giving birth to a ram; beneath her are three bulls' heads with auroch horns. The Goddess in the same birth-giving position yields a bull with spreading horns, modeled in clay and plastered (VIB 8); a second bull, this one painted with auroch's horns, was probably once mounted on the wall. The Goddess herself faced four sets of horns. The horn as symbol permeates the shrines: a row of auroch horns decorates a bench in another sacred room. The horn had been a sacred symbol since the Paleolithic, as the Venus of Laussel reminds us; at Çatal Hüyük, the horns are preeminent symbols of regeneration seen in association with both symbols of death and those of burgeoning life (the birthing Goddess herself and symbols of the life force, triangles, double triangles, and eggs among them).[11]

The sacral nature of relief and painting is indicated by the fact that they occurred in shrines, not in parts of houses designated for living, and by the practice of plastering over the images or, alternatively, breaking the face, hands, and feet of the Goddess or the animal head, rendering the power of the image inutile when the shrine was no longer in use. The presence of handprints on certain of the images, made by dipping the hand in red paint, bears testimony to a ritual involving touch: the handprint of a small child appears on the body of a Goddess in one place, while adult hands appear on bulls' and rams' heads.[12] At Çatal Hüyük the parietal representations of the Goddess have no sexual characteristics save a large, prominent navel; sometimes she is dressed, and although she is faceless one mural shows her with long, flowing hair.[13] The navel of the Goddess resembles the protruding navel of late pregnancy. She is often surrounded with symbols of her gifts and powers, including net patterns relating to weaving.

The Goddess' command of the fauna of the sacred landscape is indicated in sculptures, reliefs, and paintings by the flanking leopards who support her in birth; by the leopard cubs who rest on the shoulders of a seated Goddess rendered in clay; by a painted clay statuette showing the Goddess in a leopard-skin garment. A statuette of a boy riding a leopard may represent the Goddess' son or consort. Painted leopards in relief stand face-to-face on a shrine wall (VIB 44); they bear many coats of paint and plaster, testifying to the image's long sacral use. Also found in this shrine, in addition to grains, statuettes, and stalactites, were a red painted bull's head and the remains of a bucranium.

The Goddess of Çatal Hüyük also presided over the forces of vegetation, as evidenced by the statuettes of the Goddess found in grain bins and by floral patterns in the shrines, as well as honeycombs, chrysalises, bees, and butterflies, often in combination with paintings of the human hand. The human hand and its print as connected to sacred rite had been part of humanity's heritage since the caves of the Paleolithic; with the advent of an agricultural society, the hand that sowed, planted, and reaped would gain in symbolic intensity. At Çatal Hüyük, hands are found in conjunction with honeycombs and nets, bulls' heads, and fields of flowers.[14]

The accomplishments of the society of Çatal Hüyük belie their place in time: here, the world's first textiles were woven; here obsidian was polished to a mirrorlike sheen without a single scratch; here lead and copper were smelted. The city traded with regions farther south, as the discovery of cowrie shells from the Red Sea and dentalium, whelks, and cockles from the Mediterranean attests. Bowls, cosmetic palettes, axes of greenstone, and other objects reflect sophisticated techniques of grinding and polishing stone, as does the multiplicity of grave goods, all of them objects from daily life.

The civilization of Çatal Hüyük was not destroyed but simply came to an end when the site was abandoned for another, as yet unexcavated, on the other side of the river. The close connection between the symbols of the Goddess as she was realized at Çatal Hüyük and the sacred landscape over which she reigned reminds us that the religion of the Neolithic is firmly rooted in the earth.

From Achilleion in Greece, part of the Neolithic Sesklo culture of Thessaly, comes another vision of the Goddess, one strongly tied to the agricultural activities of its people. The site was continuously occupied from the mid-seventh millennium B.C., and its culture, which shows an autonomous and continuous development throughout its history, lasted close to one thousand years. While the Goddess of Achilleion is primarily the Goddess of the Grain, she also takes on the most important of the Neolithic epiphanies: the Bird Goddess, the Snake Goddess, the Birth-giving Goddess, the Frog Goddess of Regeneration, the Pregnant Goddess, the Nurse, as well as the aspect of a male god. At Achilleion, she does not appear as the Goddess of Death but is instead connected to "life creation, birth-giving, health protection, increase, fertility of humans, animals, fields and plants, and the seasonal return of life powers."[15] According to Marija Gimbutas, the excavator of the site, neither funerals nor burials at Achilleion were ritualized.

The settlement was on the rise of a hillside overlooking a small river, a perennial source of water; the valley around it was covered with oak and pistachio groves. The plain of Thessaly was wetter and cooler than it is now, and the environment was in many ways optimal. Oak groves provided the habitat for wild fauna: red deer, auroch, wild swine, fox, hare, wildcat, badger, as well as birds. Other wild arbors yielded seasonal fruits, nuts, and berries. Not surprisingly, the setting's economy was largely based on agriculture and animal husbandry (domesticated sheep, goats, cattle, pigs, and dogs), although the earth also provided local sources of greenstone and red jasper for a lithic industry that produced agricultural and woodworking tools as well as ceremonial greenstone axes.

The Goddess at Achilleion formed a part of the rhythms of daily life. As Marija Gimbutas noted, the locations of figurines and cult vessels in house shrines or in the workshop of the shrines, in the open courtyards at the oven or hearth or at the bench nearby, in the ritual and garbage pits, make it clear that they were "literally omnipresent" inside and outside the houses. All human activities, the grinding of grain, the making of bread, the weaving of cloth, "were inseparable from the participation of the divine."[16] Different epiphanies of the Goddess apparently served different ritual and human needs. The Pregnant Goddess, sometimes masked, often enthroned, was found in and associated with the activities of the courtyard, especially those related to the making of bread. At a large circular hearth were found not only a sacrificial table and the leg of a vessel but a figurine in the birth-giving position with a prominently modeled vulva. The Snake Goddess and the Bird Goddess were used ritually or worshipped within the house shrines, on altars or at a protected hearth; they appear to be related to the domestic sphere, as they would later be in Minoan civilization. The existence of spouted vases and other vessels suggests that libations were part of ceremonies within the houses; the discovery of two bone tubes, presumably pipes, inside two houses near figurines and sacrificial tables suggests that music also was a part of ritual. Pottery decorated with sacred signs such as *v*'s, chevrons, and triangles suggests their use in sacral rites.

Of the two hundred figurines found at Achilleion, only two could tentatively be identified as male; images of phalluses, perhaps used as standing pillars or as figurine heads, were found, possibly connoting energy. But it is overwhelmingly the Pregnant Goddess, the Goddess of the Grain, of the circular hearth and oven, and of bread, whose dominion over the land and life was proclaimed by the rich fields of the Thessaly Plain, and who is at the center of the Neolithic religion of Achilleion.

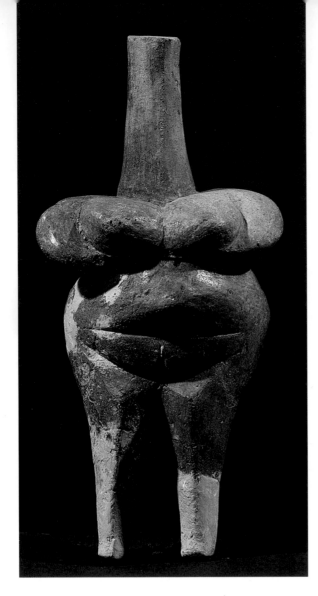

OPPOSITE PAGE: **Stiff Nudes from Krasno, Bulgaria**

LEFT: **Goddess from the Hamangia Culture, Romania** (c. 5000 B.C.)

Found in a grave in the Cernavoda cemetery—which contained more than four hundred burials—this is the Goddess in her aspect of death, what Marija Gimbutas called the "Stiff Nude." In this culture the dead were buried in an extended position, accompanied by sculptures in a seated or standing position, as well as flat-backed Goddesses placed lying down. Other grave goods included a flat ax, pots, marble or shell ornaments, symbolic tools, and other grave offerings. The Hamangian Goddess of the grave is always faceless, her head indicated by a phallic column; her breasts, prominent hips, and pubic triangle promise fertility and rebirth.

The Cernavoda cemetery also yielded two masked figures, one a sorrowing male and the other female, which Marija Gimbutas suggests may represent the Dying God of vegetation and the Earth Mother.

RIGHT: **Goddess from Tell Azmak, Bulgaria** (Early Sixth Millennium)

The dominance of her pubic triangle tells us that she is the great Goddess of Life and Regeneration. Carved of marble, which N. K. Sandars suggests came from the Aegean, she reminds us that the Goddess of the Cyclades had her roots in Old Europe.

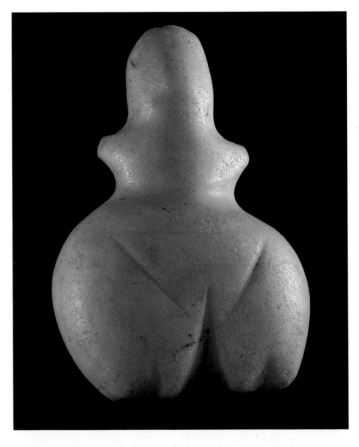

Perhaps the most singular, mysterious, and awe-inspiring landscape of the Neolithic was that which surrounded the community of Lepenski Vir, in what became Yugoslavia, on the banks of the Danube. It is not surprising that this sacred landscape yielded a vision of the Goddess that was allied to the other traditions of the Neolithic, but it also possessed a special stamp. This community settled first on the water's edge, next to the great, swirling whirlpool that gives the area its name (*vir* means "whirlpool"), and then moved slightly inland on the horseshoe-shaped shelf that lies between the right bank of the Danube and the steep cliffs of the Korso hills. The landscape here was an extreme compression of the forces of nature in their full range, from life-giving to life-threatening. On the one hand, the forest was full of fruit-bearing trees and game and the river full of fish, a nearly inexhaustible food supply. The swift but predictable currents in the river made fishing extremely easy, since the fish were driven by the water and could be trapped in the shallows by waiting fishermen.[17] The raised terrace of the shelf provided respite from the winds and the flooding waters of the Danube. Ores, minerals, shells, and snails were easily accessible when the water level in the Danube lowered, and there were plentiful and various rocks, gray-green sandstone, reddish limestone, granite, serpentine, porphyrite, and red sandstone among them. Yet the swirling danger of the *vir* was always present, as was the thunderous sound of the Danube flowing downstream; from the Korso hills, there was the danger of rock slides. Above the settlement the Carpathian Mountains encircled the river, and clouds and mists on their peaks must have added to the sense of physical isolation and danger. Across from the settlement, on the left side of the Danube, a huge barren cliff some 2,200 feet high rose out of the earth; and over it, each morning, the sun climbed.

The isolation of the settlement marked its life. According to the excavator, the first four levels of settlement contained not a single object gathered from more than a day's journey away.[18] The shelf on which Lepenski Vir stood was a mere 550 feet long by 165 feet wide, bounded by the turbulent Danube on one side and the forest and cliffs on the other, suggesting a community of physical and psychic dependence. It was a hermetic existence, yielding rite, practice, and symbol unlike any other.

The houses at Lepenski Vir were of a standard shape, which was maintained throughout the generations for roughly a thousand years: trapezoidal structures, triangles with their tops sheared off, with entrances facing the river. The floors of the houses were made of red limestone and clay, the roofs of wood. Through successive stages of building, the interiors of the houses became more standardized, suggesting a closely knit society bound by codified rules and rituals. Set off from the living quarters was a rectangular hearth surrounded by a row of red upright triangles. Beyond the hearth were stone "tables," which set the sacral area off from the living quarters without a physical barrier. Next to the hearth stood an altar that consisted of a boulder broader than it was tall, able to stand upright, with a depression in its center, and one or two sculptures carved out of grainy limestone, yellow in color with red patches. The boulders out of which the sculptures were made were specially gathered from a river some six miles away from Lepenski Vir, a place undoubtedly endowed with sacred meaning, and were chosen for both their shape and their size, since the size of the sculpture corresponds to the dimensions of the space for which it was intended.[19] Sunk into the floor, these sculptures are of extraordinary quality: one depicts a woman, while others clearly bear the faces of fish but with breasts or with the pubic triangle inscribed. They range from only six to twenty inches in height, but are nonetheless monumental in their effect. In one of the houses, a red painted sculpture had an inscribed vulva, shown in the open, final stages of birth. Others of the rounded sculptures, resembling heads, were carved with labyrinthine motifs, chevrons, and spirals: symbols of the Goddess in her aspect of regeneration. A fragment of a deer horn, an animal that also represents the Goddess of rebirth and that was of symbolic importance at Lepenski Vir, was incised with triangles, chevrons, and parallel zigzag lines, the last emblematic of water. One altar is shaped in the head of a fish, perhaps a carp, and two others resemble the form of a deer; still others are inscribed with labyrinthine motifs, and some were left totally undecorated. Aniconic boulders, mostly uncarved, were also given important positions within the sanctuaries, contemporaneous with and often next to carved boulders, indicating that they too were possessed of power and sacrality.[20]

At Lepenski Vir the bodies of the dead were first excarnated, perhaps hung in the trees of the forest where birds of prey and insects could strip away the flesh. A single grave from the earliest stages of settlement, bearing the skeleton of a man, was dug in the shape of a triangle facing the river, thus echoing the shape and orientation of the houses. Dragoslav Srejović, the excavator of Lepenski Vir, suggests a connection between the position of the sacred boulders in the home and the position of the human skull within the grave: each is placed in the western corner of the triangle, and each faces east, where the sun would rise over the high bare cliff.[21] That such a connection exists is shown by later, related burial practices: first individual bones and then later complete skeletons were buried within the sanctuary area of the houses, in front of or behind the hearth. The dead were aligned so that their hands touched the hearth on one side and the holy boulder on the other. Stag antlers and sometimes stag skulls were regularly placed with the remains. Once the dead were buried within, the structure was abandoned as habitation, but continued to serve as a place of burial.[22]

The Fish Goddess of Lepenski Vir reigned over not only the rites of the dead but

Fish Goddesses from Lepenski Vir

In the image on the right, the naturally rounded stone gives way to breasts, vulva, and schematized hands; next to it, as it was found in the sanctuary where it stood, is a smaller sculpture showing only the head with facial features. The statue's anthropomorphic features combine with its clearly fishlike elements to give it a grave solemnity, befitting the image of one who presided not only over the fish-filled river of life but over the mysterious whirlpool that animated the waters.

56

also those of rebirth, symbolized by the triangular forms echoed throughout the structures, the vulva and other carvings pecked out of the stones, and the red coloration, emblem of life. The triangular shapes of the "houses" of the dead echo the triangles that the living inhabited, suggesting a connection between those two realms contained within the Goddess' sphere. Animal sacrifice was practiced at Lepenski Vir; the bones of fish, deer, dogs, and wild boars were found in all the sanctuaries. Marija Gimbutas has noted that while dogs and boars are attendants to the Goddess of death, the red deer and the fish represent her aspect of rebirth.[23] The signs carved on the altars, concentric circles, cruciforms, and zigzags, among others, were not merely decorative but were meant to invoke the Goddess, a fact made clear by their appearance on both visible surfaces and those buried beneath the floor of the sanctuary. The power of these symbols of invocation aligns the rites of Lepenski Vir with those as far away in time and distance as the burial at La Ferrassie and the sacred structures of Malta and New Grange in Ireland.

While the red color, the spiral, the eye, and the labyrinth, all signs and symbols of the Goddess at Lepenski Vir, are those of the Neolithic era elsewhere, here her epiphany as Fish is again closely linked to this fantastic landscape. She was portrayed as a denizen of the swirling, turbulent river, replete with the food of life and the essence of danger, that formed one of the boundaries of their world. The end of the culture at Lepenski Vir is as silent, as mysterious, as its beginning: from the dark sand that covered all, from sacred hearths to sculptúres, the excavators deduced that the site had been suddenly abandoned and, for a time, left uninhabited. Those who came after appeared to know nothing of the past, of the fishlike Goddess or the sacred triangular shapes. They dug random caves into the shelf or built semisubterranean houses, and buried their dead in shallow graves devoid of orientation or order. Only the whirlpool remained, still holding its grip on the fast-flowing water, as it does today.

Images of the Neolithic Goddess from other areas, other cultures, remind us of her multiplicity and of the increasing complexity of sacral tradition. It is difficult to look at these images without mourning the loss of the mythology that made them represent the cosmic whole, a mythology that can only be reconstructed and imagined by a process of analogy. The Vinča culture of the central Balkans, which lasted from 5300 to 4300 B.C., comprised more than 650 separate settlements, on or near rivers. The eponymous settlement is some eight and a half miles east of Belgrade, but the culture stretched to Bosnia in the southwest, eastward to western Bulgaria, and to southwestern Romania. While the fertility of the land and the potential for farming dictated the location of the

Ritual Objects from Ovcharov, Bulgaria
(Mid-Fifth Millennium)

The four figurines are inscribed with *v*'s, meanders, streams, and parallel lines, identifying them as Bird Goddesses. The sacred objects include altar screens painted with red symbols on both sides, miniature tables and chairs, and lidded vessels. The presence of three drums connects the scene to the ritual use of music. Marija Gimbutas has suggested that this miniature tableau may, in fact, replicate an actual ritual for the Bird Goddess.

Found with these ritual objects was a clay model of a temple with a house-shaped oven and a bench or altar, enclosed by a clay wall. The exterior wall of the temple had been painted with sacred symbols, chevrons and tri-lines among them.

settlements on flat river terraces or on gently sloping foothills, they were "frequently near streams, brooks, or thermal waters considered holy to this day."[24] Selevac, a Vinča settlement that was inhabited from 5000 to 4400 B.C., was located on a stream but was less than six miles away from the Morava River, which ultimately meets the Danube, an important confluence.[25]

The Vinča culture was an indigenous one, and its growth in the arts, in the material culture, and in religion was uninterrupted for one thousand years. The Goddess as she is realized here connotes formal ritual, as a numinous presence beyond the human. She is, from the beginning, masked. Even the mask itself, symbol of a supernatural deity, perhaps indicating one whose face could not be looked on directly by human eyes, had its own evolution in typology. The mask became increasingly formalized: a rough triangular form became a triangular one, then an undecorated pentagonal shape (mid-Vinča), then a decorated pentagonal form with semicircular eyes, and finally fully decorated in a pictorial style with almond, slanting eyes.[26] The presence of monumental life-size masks at Vinča sites in what was southern Yugoslavia suggests dramatic or ceremonial rituals, with human beings taking on roles in the sacred mythology. From this area too come extraordinary sculptures of masked human heads with bulls' bodies, called centaurs; at Valac, whole or fragmentary centaurs, decorated with red crusted paint, were found on or under floors.[27]

Of the Goddess' many manifestations in the Vinča culture, the masked Bird Goddess predominates; inscribed or painted on the sculptures are the symbols that associate the Goddess with the moisture of life, water, as well as powers of regeneration: v's, chevrons, meanders, and triangles among them. At several Vinča sites, the vast majority of figurines were painted red, symbolic of the regenerative power.[28] The Vinča Goddess has other epiphanies as well, each of them recognizable yet distinct, including a bear mother and a Snake Goddess. Male figures wearing ram or goat masks (constituting nearly one-fifth of the figurines) and zoomorphic figurines and vessels of snakes, frogs, hedgehogs, dogs, and fish form a part of the sacred Vinča mythology. Even though the houses and possible sacred areas of the Vinča culture are hard to distinguish from each other, Marija Gimbutas suggests that certain multiroomed houses were sacral areas, clearly distinguished from areas of habitation by painted walls and symbolic designs such as chevrons and meanders, painted in red, blue, and white.[29] At Anza in Macedonia, excavated by Gimbutas, the sheer number of bird-shaped and anthropomorphic vases with protrusions (called protomes) in the shape of horned animals found on the Vinča level suggested a shrine.[30] Alternatively, John Chapman has argued that Vinča life was permeated with ritual activity and that an ever-widening range of activities and tasks were

LEFT: **Goddess and Child, Vinča Culture, Drenovac, Yugoslavia**

The Goddess is the protectress of young life, as this figure reminds us. Her masked face tells us forcefully that she and her young are numinous, but the protective cradle of her arm announces that she is indeed nurse and mother to all life.

Temple Model from Vinča Culture, Romania (C. 5200–5000 B.C.)

Marija Gimbutas has identified this model as depicting the Goddess' realm as that of water, symbolized by the incised meanders, which were inlaid with white; entrance to her realm is gained by a door at the bottom. The head of the Goddess, shown in reconstruction in this photograph, identifies her as the Bird Goddess of creation.

61

Seated Goddess, Vinča Culture, Carsija, Yugoslavia (c. 4700–4500 B.C.)

The V-shaped emblem around her neck identifies her as a Goddess, as does the ritual costume she wears: a hip belt and a dotted apron with fringes. The holes in the apron are filled in with white; made of clay, she is fired nearly black.

Altar Table, Early Vinča, Fafos I, Yugoslavia

Meanders painted red are incised on this altar table in the shape of an animal-masked woman. The legs appear to be those of a bear or a bull.

associated with ritual objects, connected not simply to the house but to open-air ceremonies as well. The existence of pits containing ritual objects has suggested communal outdoor activities. At Tartaria in west Romania, twenty-six fired-clay figurines, two alabaster figurines, a fired-clay anchor, a Spondylus bracelet, and three clay plaques with signs and symbols were deposited with human bones.[31]

As elsewhere, the horns of the bull and the ox were an important religious symbol of regeneration. At four Vinča sites, clay-covered ox skulls were found attached to clay columns or walls; blue paint covered their muzzles; on their foreheads, red triangles had been painted. The presence, too, of hundreds of small horned stands from Vinča sites, each with a hole between the horns for the insertion of a sacral image, suggests that horns were associated with a "myth-enacting ceremony."[32] At Anza, vases with horned animals or animal protomes were found with beaked figurines, as well as a red painted ram's head with three spiraling horns. A terra-cotta horned stand with breasts, from Smederervska Palanka in Serbia, reminds us that while the Indo-Europeans and their sky-god religion regarded the bull as masculine, the traditions of Old Europe allied the sacred horns with the powers of the Goddess.

The sacred image of the Goddess of Old Europe is an intricate tapestry, composed of many-colored threads woven by different hands, but revealing an underlying consonance. The religion of the Goddess was integral to and integrated in Old European life: the Goddess presided over birth and death, as we see at Çatal Hüyük, but she also presided over all that lies between. The religion of the Goddess permeated the everyday, blurring the distinction between ordinary and sacral activity. It seems probable that the figurines and vessels represented a larger mythology now lost to us, and that ritual ceremonies were enacted by individuals and on a communal basis, both within the houses and outside of them. The Goddess as she was realized in these cultures was as multiplicious as the natural world she encompassed, a world where the fate of humanity was interwoven with the forces of nature.

**Bird Goddess, Vinča
Culture** (c. 4500–4000 B.C.)

4 The Flowering of the Goddess

The first incursions of the early Indo-Europeans or, as Marija Gimbutas has called them, Kurgans into east central Europe between 4400 and 4300 B.C. began to change the culture and spirituality of Old Europe. These people brought with them not only a religion of sky gods but a culture based on equine mobility, a hierarchical society, and a militant patriarchy.[1] However, the religion of the Goddess continued to flourish in the southern extremities of the continent, most notably on islands in the Mediterranean and the Aegean, including Sicily, Sardinia, the Cyclades, Malta, and Crete. In these places, most of them isolated from the mainland by water yet, in later millennia, in contact with each other, the roots of Old Europe yielded the Goddess in full bloom for more than three thousand years. Although much of the surviving archaeological evidence from the Aegean and Mediterranean is funerary in origin, and thus emphasizes the Goddess in her chthonic aspects, she doubtless presided over all of life.

A holy cave in southeastern Italy reminds us that the flowering of the Goddess begins deep in the earth and far back in time. The Scaloria Cave, near present-day Manfredonia, is composed of two caves: the upper, which contained evidence of tools and possibly habitation, is wide, while the lower one has stalagmites and a live spring. Marija Gimbutas' excavations of the site show that ceremonies were conducted here in the mid-sixth millennium (5600–5300 B.C.) near the "water of life"; shards from more than fifteen hundred vases were decorated with symbols of the Goddess in her aspect of regeneration, among them triangles, snakes, plants, suns, and *v*'s.[2] At the entrance to the cave, skeletons were found buried, suggesting that indeed the ceremonies involved regeneration. The continued worship of the Goddess in caves, particularly those with stalagmites (earth pillars of the Goddess symbolizing the life force), connects this site to the ancient ways of the Paleolithic and to Çatal Hüyük.

Unlike many of the islands in the Mediterranean, Sicily has been inhabited since the Paleolithic era, when humans settled in the rock shelters and caves in the cliffs of the island's shores. The largest of the Mediterranean islands, it has both mountains and fertile plains; in the Paleolithic, it supported a variety of flora and fauna, and the surrounding waters supplied vast numbers of mollusks easily gathered from the shores, as the large number of shells from the period found in the habitation levels of caves attest. But the Sicilian landscape is also defined by potent symbols of nature's chthonic power and of the Goddess. Its highest peak is Mount Etna, while the nearby Lipari Islands — Lipari, Salina,

The Island of Thera, the Cyclades

Vulcano, Stromboli — are all volcanic. The portrait of these islands in the Homeric epics and in later Greek myth evokes the physical dangers and violence inherent in the natural landscape as well as identifying it as sacred to the Goddess. The Strait of Messina, which separates Sicily from the mainland, was home to the mythological female monsters Scylla and Charybdis. Scylla, a six-headed sea monster who dwelt in the cliffs and whose body below the waist is encased in a cave, snatched unwary sailors from passing ships. Charybdis was a bottomless whirlpool who dwelt under another, lower cliff and who sucked the waters in and spouted them up three times a day. They were to plague the journeys of two heroes of the new patriarchal order, Odysseus and Jason, and thus probably represent sites that were once consecrated to the powers of the Goddess. Sicily was thought to be home to the cave-dwelling Cyclops, who presents Odysseus with an extraordinary challenge, key to his heroic identity. Aeolus, the god of the winds, who also plays a part in the journey of Odysseus, was thought to live in the Liparis, once called the Aeolians. Hephaestos, the lame Olympian god of fire and metallurgy who created Pandora, was thought to be born on Vulcano.

Paleolithic remains on Sicily echo findings at sites elsewhere. The cave of San Teodoro revealed three burials, all of them covered with red ocher; one grave contained a pendant of deer teeth, and another a deer antler.[3] Painted and incised figures in caves on Sicily and the smaller surrounding islands indicate that here too certain caves were places of rite and sacrality. A cave on the island of Levanso contained parietal incised art depicting both animals and anthropomorphic figures, as well as a bovid incised on a stone and two pebbles painted with lines of red ocher. Near Palermo on the north coast of Sicily, on the slopes of Monte Pellegrino, are the Addaura caves and several shelters. These caves, situated high above precipitous cliffs, have extraordinary incised art that appears to show a number of ritual scenes.[4] The interpretation of these scenes, located in their womblike sanctuary, has been the subject of much scholarly debate. The first scene, which does not appear to be composed, shows animals, including a mare with a colt and a running deer, as well as what may be a woman with a swollen belly, and two males. One of the men is wearing a bird mask. The second scene, more deeply incised into the rock, shows two men with erect phalluses lying prone, bound neck to ankle; around them circle five men, some of them bird-masked, some with their arms raised or half raised. Carved below this scene on the rock wall are other male figures, these seen in conjunction with deer. Reminiscent of the bird-masked male at Lascaux carved into the Shaft of the cave, this is surely an image of sacred ritual, although its precise meaning eludes us. Is the Addaura tableau an image of a sacred dance in the Goddess' womb or perhaps a mock sacrifice insuring the continuation of the life force?[5] Or an initiation?[6]

**Rock Tomb,
Agrigento, Sicily**

The advent of the Neolithic era in Sicily is marked by the Stentinello culture (named after the village near Syracuse first excavated in the 1890s) and by an influx of new settlers who brought with them agricultural skills; the disruption of the Paleolithic and Mesolithic traditions of flint working on the island indicates a break with the older tradition of the first inhabitants. These new settlers no longer lived in caves but built villages that were often fortified; it is unclear whether they were protecting themselves from the first Sicilian settlers or the arrival of newcomers in search of arable land. Obsidian from the volcanic island of Lipari provided them with the basis of trade. Stentinello pottery is decorated with lozenges, eye motifs, spirals, and meanders. The eyes of the Goddess, symbol of the divine source and also emblem of the Goddess in her aspect of death, continue to figure in the sacral expression of Sicily.[7] Figurines of the Goddess were no more than pebbles with vulvae and breasts incised on them — versions of the stiff white Goddess in her aspect of death. The single grave found from the Stentinello culture was oval, surrounded by and paved with slabs of stone.

It is in the cultures of the Copper Age and early Bronze Age of Sicily that the image of the Goddess comes more clearly into focus. Burial practices change: the stone chist or slab was abandoned for tombs cut into rock, as in Sardinia and elsewhere. Near the village of San Cono, situated on the top of a hill, two tombs illustrate the transition: one is a round grave with irregular slabs, while the second is an oven-type tomb opening off a cylindrical shaft. From the Conca d'Oro culture in northwestern Sicily (the present-day provinces of Palermo and Trapani) come oval or rounded tombs, opening out from a vertical shaft; sometimes the shaft leads to two or three cells, each with a diameter between three and six feet. The dead, covered in red ocher, were buried here with grave goods. Not surprisingly, the sacred symbols of the Goddess, already established in the Stentinello culture, continued to decorate pottery and grave goods. Terra-cotta horns were also found on the sites, notably at Sant'Ippolito.[8]

From the early Bronze Age (3000–2500 B.C.) comes the Castelluccio culture. The eponymous village was at the top of a rock spur with deep valleys on either side of it, thus isolating and protecting the site from its surroundings. Several hundred rock tombs are cut into the limestone cliffs of a side valley. They are small, oval-shaped rooms, some with an anteroom, and in each of them were numerous inhumations. The entryways to these tombs, two and a half to three feet tall, were closed by stone slabs decorated with regenerative spirals formed into occuli motifs, indicating the presence of the Goddess in her aspect of death. Rams' horns, identified throughout Old Europe with the Bird Goddess, also occur.[9] The Castelluccio tombs yielded elongated objects fashioned out of bone, again inscribed with sacred symbols. One tomb in the Castelluccio complex incorporated four pillars in its hallway, while another at Cava Lazzaro was built with an imitation architectural facade of pillars. These architectural imitations may well have connected the precincts of the dead with the sacred sites of the living, as they did in Sardinia and Malta.

Both Sardinia's location and its physical terrain presented a remarkable set of circumstances. Along with Corsica, less than eight miles away at its northern tip, Sardinia sat directly on the route for sea traffic between the central and western parts of the Mediterranean. It is an extremely mountainous island, with granitic peaks in the east and volcanic mountains in the west, the latter the source of the highly prized obsidian that formed the basis for Sardinia's trade.[10] It was first settled at the end of the seventh millennium by mariners from Tuscany, though the culture would not truly flourish until several thousand years later. The results, while highly varied, are evidence of what has been called an "unbroken cultural sequence."[11]

The first settlers lived in caves, and although they knew the arts of agriculture, they subsisted largely by hunting, fishing, and raising animals. During the middle of the fifth millennium, the land was increasingly farmed, and villages were established as the old caves of habitation were abandoned. Excavations by David Trump at two sites in the Bonu Ighinu valley in northwestern Sardinia attest to the continuity of ritual traditions even as these changes took place.[12] The two sites are caves located on the side of a valley overhung by the cliffs of Monte Traessu. The cave of Su Tintirriolu — known as Ucca de Su Tintirriolu or "Mouth of the Bats" — is difficult to reach, for a portion of its entrance passage is a mere twenty-eight inches between floor and ceiling. Inside the entrance, five shaped blocks of stone or rough stelae indicate that this was a ritual site, as does the presence of points of obsidian and flint, terra-cotta figurines, and large quantities of pottery.[13] Human bones were found here too. Deep within the cave were stalagmitic formations, ancient and enduring symbols of the Goddess within the earth. Trump's discovery of a second cave 380 yards downstream from Su Tintirriolu, called the Grotta di Filestru, clarifies the history of the sacral cave. Airy, spacious, and light, with a perennial spring outside of its entrance, the Filestru Cave was a cave of habitation. As Trump explains it, Filestru was the "village" and Tintirriolu was the sacred cave. In the second period, the village moved to Monte Noe, the mountain that looks over the entire heart of the Bonu Ighinu basin, while sacral activity continued at Su Tintirriolu.[14] Archaeological evidence shows that the cave remained an active ritual site during the later Ozieri period, which also saw the building of egg-shaped rock-cut tombs in the neighboring area, many of their walls still stained with red ocher. Whatever artifacts were in these tombs have long since disappeared, and any evidence of the rites that connected the cave and the tombs no longer exists.

As Marija Gimbutas has demonstrated, the egg or oven shape is a symbol of regeneration in the culture of Old Europe.[15] The Sardinian tombs are cut into the rock face or into the ground, with either long or short entrances. At the tomb of Cuccuru S'Arriu, a rounded figurine of the Goddess, her belly and her pubic triangle melding together, was placed before a body buried in the fetal position and covered by red ocher. Two valves of an opened shell, a symbol of the vulva which dates back to the Paleolithic, were also found filled with red ocher. The Goddess figures of this period, carved of alabaster or soft rock, are rounded.[16] These egg-shaped tombs and their artifacts form the basis for sacred sites of increasing complexity during the Ozieri culture (c. 4000 B.C.), so named for a sacral cave, San Michele, discovered at the beginning of this century near Ozieri. The cave of San Michele seems to testify to ritual practices that are rooted in the ancient, like those at Su Tintirriolu. An irregular limestone cavern, San Michele has an entrance requiring a twenty-foot drop into a main chamber, which leads in turn to a smaller one. After the small chamber, the cave becomes a labyrinth of crannies. Along with red ocher, a green-stone-ax amulet, and a limestone pebble inscribed with what seem to be eyes and striations, Ozieri pottery was found, inscribed with triangles, zigzags, and circles, the patterns emphasized by red or white filling. The cave's entrance was blocked by a six-foot-tall slab, which, in addition to its difficult access and the presence of a skull and bones, suggests that this was a place of rite.[17] At Anghelu Ruju, dating from the same period, more than thirty-five tombs were discovered, varying from simple chambers to large ones with smaller chambers radiating off them. Some of these tombs are decorated with carved bulls' heads in relief, placed above and next to the squared door; the doorways themselves are sometimes carved in imitation of wood, with a lintel. On occasion, bulls' heads are also carved on sandstone pillars within the tomb. The heads have often been painted with ocher, connecting the symbolism of regeneration — the egg shape of the tomb, the horns — back in time to Çatal Hüyük and forward in time to the horns of consecration at the palaces of Minoan Crete. At S. Andrea Priu, what was once a group of some twenty tombs was carved into a vertical cliff. While landslides have destroyed the majority, those tombs remaining reveal fascinating renderings in rock of architectural features of wood: roof beams, rafters, and pilasters. Like the Hal Saflieni Hypogeum of Malta, which is later in date, these features indicate a connection between the burial places of the dead and the sacred places of the living, and suggest that these were not simply tombs but places of ritual or temples. Other sites attest to further incorporation of the details of a sacred architecture. At Noeddale, three single-chamber tombs were found, one with a funerary

Tomb at S. Andrea Priu, Bonorva, Sardinia

The rock has been hewn to imitate rafters and beams; recesses for burials are on the sides. While some of the rock-cut tombs of Sardinia are single egg-shaped rooms, these are multichambered.

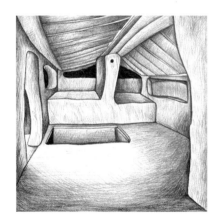

**Rock-Cut Tomb,
Bonorva, Sardinia**

alcove cut into the rock as well as votive pits hewn out of the center of the floor. The fourth tomb had eight chambers; in one, the roof supports of a circular hut were imitated in stone.[18] These sacred structures in stone were often painted and decorated with red: at Busachi, the portal was surrounded by red painted incisions in the rock and a red circle was painted on the ceiling of an antechamber.

At Is Araus, two pairs of breasts and a face were carved on the slab closing the portal to the tomb.[19] The life-giving breasts were also connected in the Ozieri culture to the eyes of the Goddess as a divine source: a terra-cotta figurine from the early fourth millennium has eyes engraved over the breasts.[20] Signs and symbols of the Goddess in her aspect of regeneration decorated the interiors of many of the Sardinian hypogea: at

Goddess from Sernobi, Sardinia (Fifth Millennium)

This Sardinian Goddess is highly schematized, her facial features reduced to a nose, her rigid breasts highly separated, surmounted by a V. Made of marble, this figure of the Goddess in her aspect of death probably stood out in the open.

72

the entrance to a tomb at Pimental, red carved spirals and triangles with spirals appear. A relief on a rock-cut tomb at Perfugas shows a huge ram's head with an owl's beak, a hybrid form of the Bird Goddess and her sacred animal, the ram.[21] The Goddess as she is realized in the Ozieri culture becomes schematized as an emblem of death and regeneration: no longer rounded but flat, she is faceless save for a beaklike nose, wears a V-shaped collar, and has prominent breasts. Her lower body is an undifferentiated cone. Ozieri pottery, in myriad vessel and vase forms, displays not only the symbols of the Goddess — snakes, chevrons, triangles, occuli, suns — but also apparently mythical scenes that may indicate rites. A ritual vessel from Serra Is Araus shows two figures, their heads indicated by radiating suns, their bodies by parallel lines, their feet by birds' claws.[22]

Certainly the most extraordinary and mysterious sacred site of this Sardinian culture is Monte D'Accoddi, an artificial tumulus built of earth and stones, revetted with huge blocks of limestone, one inset slightly above the other, to form a roughly pyramidal shape. On the south side of the construction, a trapeze-shaped ramp leads upward to the summit, which stood some ten meters aboveground. Found at Monte D'Accoddi were greenstone axes; loom weights (some of them pyramidal in form); bone objects; Goddess figurines; and large amounts of pottery, tripods and pots among them, decorated with triangles, concentric circles, zigzags, single and double spirals. One vessel found here shows five figures, their upper and lower bodies indicated by joined triangles forming hourglass shapes; the figures' hands are linked, perhaps showing a ritual dance. Surrounding Monte D'Accoddi are large menhirs and standing stones, and nearby are the rock-cut tombs of Su Crucifissu, Marinaru, and Ponte Secco.[23]

What rites took place here on Monte D'Accoddi's flattened top? Can we imagine a procession leading up its ramp? Was this, as Marija Gimbutas opines, a place of ritual celebration, or the site of ritual excarnation?[24] Rising up out of the flat land, built by human hands, Monte D'Accoddi cannot answer.

Another vision of the Goddess emerges, far to the east, from the Cyclades. The ancient Greeks called these islands in the Aegean Sea the Kyklades, imagining them formed in a circle (*kyklos*) around the holy island of Apollo's birth, Delos. Yet, in a pattern of mythic appropriation that will be repeated elsewhere, especially on Crete, what became Apollo's sacred dominion in later ages was first holy to the Goddess. Thirty-one islands scattered over five square kilometers make up the Cyclades, with many more smaller reefs and islets. Most of these outcroppings in the sea are actually partially submerged extensions of the mountain ranges of Euboea and Attica, made of limestone and marble; only Melos,

OVERLEAF: **The Island of Delos, the Cyclades**

Thera, and their immediate neighbors are volcanic in origin. Rounded pebbles of marble can even now be found on their shores, and in millennia past, these pebbles, sometimes painted, were put into graves. The islands are a place of dazzling contrasts: white and gray rock, sometimes hidden by scrub; a sea that seems to sparkle in sunlight yet is subject to violent and sudden storms that roil its waters; a place of bright light.[25] Some islands, like Naxos, the largest of the Cyclades, have fertile plains and upland valleys as well as vegetated mountains suitable for pasture; others, like Keros, are nothing more than barren juts of rock. Melos was a source of the highly prized obsidian, which, as we know from the civilization at Çatal Hüyük, was probably endowed with symbolic properties.

Melos was most likely the first of the islands to be visited, perhaps as early as 8000 B.C., by peoples in search of obsidian.[26] The first inhabitants arrived on the tiny island of Saliagos around 5000 B.C. and settled on a promontory by the sea. There is evidence too of settlement on Antiparos, Melos, Mykonos, Naxos, and other islands, although it has been suggested that these were not permanent establishments.[27] The settlers were agricultural people who grew barley and wheat, kept livestock, hunted and fished. While no cemetery has been discovered, two tiny marble female figurines, each less than three inches high, one seated, with prominent buttocks, and the other a schematized figure in a violin shape that anticipates the "violin" figures of later millennia, attest to the early presence of the Goddess. The first cemetery at Kephala on the northern island of Kea, dating from shortly after 4000 B.C., reveals the roots of Cycladic burial practices. Below the settlement, situated on a peninsula overlooking a sheltered harbor, as are later towns of the Early Cycladic period, lay a cemetery of some forty graves built of stone and oval or rectangular in form. Some of the graves contained single burials, while others contained as many as fourteen. In addition to patterned pottery, a marble vessel was found here, as well as terra-cotta figurines that anticipate in their shapes and features the folded-arm marble Cycladic figures of a millennium later.

Life on the islands flourished, encouraged by both agricultural pursuits and the trading of the land's rich natural resources: obsidian from Melos; emery from Naxos; lead, copper, and silver from Siphnos; pumice from Thera. By 3200 B.C., Early Cycladic civilization had emerged, with its own extraordinary spiritual expression and art. Outside of the settlements, the dead were buried in trapezoidal graves, in a contracted position; the graves were banked by a retaining wall and a slab placed on top, perhaps to contain the spirits of the dead.[28] Buried with the dead are exquisitely rendered white marble figures in a wide range of sizes, allied in spirit and shape to the stiff nudes of Old Europe and those of Sardinia that precede them. While the whiteness of the marble is the color of bone and the stiffness of these sculptures echoes bone's rigidity, regenerative power is indicated by the provenance of the marble and by the carved rise of the breasts and prominently marked pubic triangles. Some of the figures are clearly pregnant, and traces of red paint in patterns and streaks suggest that the whiteness of death may have been mitigated by the regenerative color of life. The violin-shaped figures of the Goddess continued to be made and were also interred with the dead, often in large numbers.

The specific rites of religion are difficult to reconstruct, although the signs and symbols of the Goddess beckon. Ritual pottery vessels, known as "frying pans" for their similarity in shape to modern cooking equipment, were found both in settlements and in graves. They display incised symbols of the Goddess similar to carvings from other cultures: lines surrounded by triangles; spirals surrounded by triangles; a centered rayed circle surrounded by joined spirals and fish. They are all powerful symbols of regeneration, and connect the sacred art of the Cyclades to spirals at Tarxien on Malta as well as to holy places in Brittany and in Ireland. A later example of a "frying pan" from Early Cycladic II, dating from between 2700 and 2300 B.C., seems to make the symbolism almost explicit. An oared vessel without sails floats on a background of stamped concentric circles. Above the forked handle of the vessel, which resembles a pair of legs, a triangle with a vulva is incised. Marija Gimbutas notes that there are birds' feet and a fish on the prow of the ship, indicating the presence of the Goddess.[29] Other "frying pans" show simply the fish at the prow. These, combined with the vulva, are signs of regenerative power. The ceremonial ship, a symbol of renewal, is known from Brittany, Ireland, and Malta, and is a powerful image for a seafaring people, including those of the Cyclades. The presence of three lead ships in a cist grave[30] combined with two figurines of the Goddess with folded arms seems to confirm this interpretation.

Also buried with the dead were tiny bottles no more than two and a quarter inches high; they too were carved with spirals and rays, and often contained blue azurite. Cylindrical and spherical vessels known as *pyxides* (*pyxis* in the singular) are also incised with symbols of the Goddess; from the earliest cemeteries of the Early Cycladic I period are those with parallel lines and herringbone patterns. Later *pyxides*, made of chlorite schist, a greenstone, were found on Naxos, Amorgos, and Keros, and are incised with running spirals. These vessels, unlike the earlier ones, look like small roofed houses, and it has been suggested that they are temple or shrine models.[31] In the absence of surviving structures other than the cemeteries, though, little is known about Cycladic places of worship.

Pitted carvings on rocks on many of the Cycladic islands, executed largely on gray dolomitic limestone, hint at outdoor religious sites or shrines. While there are a wide variety of representations, the most common motif is either a single or double spiral, executed both on bedrock and on movable stones. The representation of the spiral, emblem of the Goddess' energy, has been found in *every* cemetery.[32] Other carvings, found on the peak of a hill on Naxos known as Korphi t'Aroniou, may point to the existence of an important shrine.[33] Here, overlooking the sea, the remains of a small elliptical stone hut were found, resting against the hollow of a rock. Ten marble slabs found here show a variety of human activities. Several depict what appear to be hunting scenes, while others are symbolic of pastoral events. On one, three figures are arranged in a rough circle with their arms raised and legs apart, perhaps in a ritual dance. Other stones show representations of boats which may be either realistic or symbolic. On one, a quadruped is on the boat while a human figure clasping the bow appears to embark. On another, two human figures appear to confront each other. Along with representations of snakes and spirals on nearby rocks and all over the island of Naxos, two closely aligned symbols of the Goddess that will find their full expression on Malta and Crete, the building and slabs led Christos Doumas to think that this was a shrine meant to invoke the deity in the realm of human activity.

Whether or not the Goddess figurines were only funerary objects has been the subject of heated scholarly debate. The fact that many of them were found broken in graves has led to speculations about whether the breakage was practical and deliberate (to fit the sculpture into a too-small grave, for example), or ritual, taking place as part of funerary rites. It has been suggested, too, that both the breakage and the evidence of repair before the object was interred indicate that the sculptures were ritual objects used in other contexts. Colin Renfrew has argued persuasively that the figures and other ritual vessels had a place outside of funerary rites, and that breakage may well have had a place in rite too, as has also been suggested by Aubrey Burl for rites in England.[34] Renfrew further speculated that the tiny island of Keros was a ritual center of the Cyclades, much as Delos would become in later millennia.

Keros, a tiny and now uninhabited infertile island, was the source of very large numbers of fragments of marble figurines, painted pottery, and marble bowls; unfortunately, the site had also been extensively looted for artifacts and what archaeological context remained was destroyed by the looters. Although archaeological excavation has not yielded any fragments of large statues, Renfrew has speculated that the monumental Cycladic figurines, many of them nearly or actually life-size, may well have been displayed on Keros for public rituals serving all of the islands.[35] Christos Doumas, too, believes that Keros was a holy island, though for an entirely different reason. By the Early Cycladic II period (2700–2300 B.C.), bones were frequently removed from graves, and new inhumations placed in them. Doumas speculates that these bones may well have been transferred to

Cycladic Goddesses

The figure at the far right was found at the cemetery of Chalandriani, on Syros. The shape of the incised pubic triangle is echoed in the triangular shapes of her body: in her shoulders, face, and breasts. Her swollen belly suggests she is pregnant, making her an eloquent and sophisticated symbol of fertility.

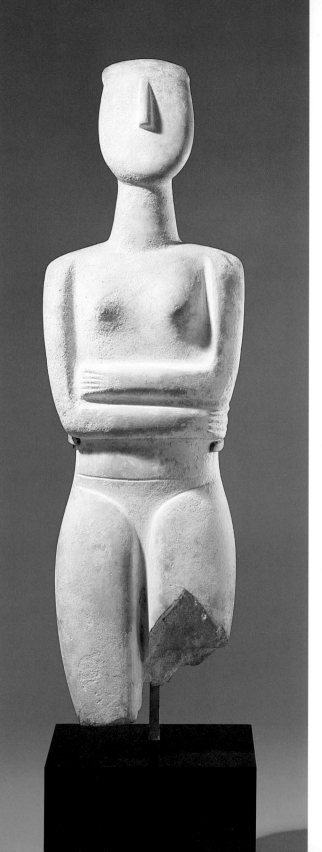

Cycladic Harpist

Was this male figure, one of several extant, meant as an offering of music in a ritual, or does it portray a votary of the Goddess?

Keros in a sacred ritual; to support his argument, he adduces the existence of a now collapsed cave on Keros containing literally thousands of marble fragments of figurines and vessels as well as human bones. Was this cave considered to be the entrance to the land of the dead, the chthonic realm, as he suggests?[36] Or was it a place of regeneration, as an earlier site on the island of Serifos had been? There, in the womb-shaped cave of Koutala, a stalagmite in the shape of a female stood in water; in front of it were burnt offerings, animal bones, and Neolithic dishes.

Other epiphanies of the Goddess from the Cyclades remind us of her multiplicity and of the continuity of the sacred symbols of Old Europe. A beautiful flat-based marble offering bowl, perhaps intended to hold grains, has a perch on which sixteen doves have landed; in Minoan Crete, the dove perches on the pillar and even on the head of the Goddess. Archaeological evidence shows that there were other such dishes.[37] Bird beads and bird pendants in stone have also been found. Pottery in bear shapes, one holding a bowl, the other a bear-shaped vessel, reminds us that in Old Europe the bear was the epiphany of the Goddess as mother and source of nurturance. Examples of the bear mother exist in cultures as various as that of Vinča, Cucuteni, and Achilleion. A magnificent marble vessel in the shape of a pig, sacred animal of the Pregnant Goddess throughout Old Europe, sacred on Minoan Crete, and even later sacred to the rites of Demeter, reminds us that the fruits of the earth on the Cyclades are in the Goddess' charge. The artifacts of the early Bronze Age Cyclades remind us as well that in the culture of Old Europe, the sun, a masculine element in the religion of the sky gods, was associated with the female Goddess: "frying pans" with radiating suns are inscribed with vulvae.

The brightness of the sun, the white of the moon, the darkness of the night sky, the alternating moods of the surrounding seas — these elements take on an intensified quality on islands. While on the one hand island life is isolated and given finite boundaries by the surrounding waters, it also encourages an independent spirit. The artifacts from these cultures transmit a sense of the elemental, of life forces as unyielding and as eternal as the rock and marble of which they are carved, and of the sky and seas that formed their boundaries. Linked and allied by a common symbolism, clearly connected to Old Europe and its roots in the Paleolithic, the nonetheless separate voices of the islands remind us of the extraordinary range of humanity's expressions.

From other holy islands, those of Malta and Gozo, come still another voice and another vision of the Goddess, and the inspiration to build eternal monuments in stone.

5 In and of the Earth: Malta

On a hillside on the island of Gozo, facing the slope, stand two megalithic temples, the Ġgantija, built in the fourth millennium and joined together by a common wall. Below lies the coast. The walls still rise in some places to a height of seventeen feet; the larger of the two edifices, the one on the south end, is a hundred feet long by a hundred feet wide. The outer walls are composed of huge slabs weighing many tons, which were rolled to the site on stone balls. Local legend has it that the Ġgantija was built in a single day and a single night by a woman nursing her child, an odd but moving variation on the creative energy of motherhood. In fact, these temples and the others that dot the islands were built over the course of hundreds of years and many generations. Sibylle von Cles-Reden has pictured the whole population working on these sacred sites, so that, like a medieval cathedral, they must have seemed symbolic of security and eternity, their monumental walls dominating the natural landscape.[1]

The Ġgantija is one of more than forty sacred structures of the Goddess on the Maltese islands. They are set apart from earlier structures by their monumental aspects and singular artistry, a level of achievement unrivaled elsewhere for another thousand years. At the same time, they reflect the architectural link to the past: built in the shape of the body of the Goddess, they belong to a tradition that stretches back to the caves.

Set against the blue waters of the Mediterranean, sixty miles from Sicily (whose snowcapped Mount Etna cools the terrain), the windswept and practically shadeless Maltese islands reflect brightness; theirs is an austere, unmitigated beauty. (Visiting Malta in the 1930s, the sybaritic D. H. Lawrence called it "bone-dry, bone-bare," "as stark as a corpse.") Today only the carob tree grows wild here in the rocky limestone soil; lakeless and riverless, the islands have topsoil that erodes easily, and rainwater washes the land into the sea. On two of these tiny islands, Malta (17.5 miles long and 8.3 miles wide) and Gozo (9 miles long and 4.5 miles wide), stood some of the greatest temples ever built by humanity to honor the Goddess, constructed on a monumental scale and in numbers that belied the dimensions of the land. Set upon hills, the temples dominated the landscape, symbols of both human effort and the larger powers that they honored. Built, rebuilt, and elaborated, they represent many generations of continuous labor and devotion, a reflection perhaps of the gratitude and honor due a deity who presided over a land that, while fertile, did not yield its fruits easily.[2] Needing to increase the amount of arable soil, the megalith builders carried soil uphill and created terraces on rocky hillsides and tops. The flowering of the prehistoric civilization of Malta lasted about seven hundred years, and ended as abruptly and mysteriously as it had begun.

Ġgantija Temples on the Island of Gozo: Massive and Corporeal

The magnificence and extent of this sacred architecture seem, like the islands themselves, oddly isolated from the outside world and impervious to outside influence, despite the probability of trade between Malta, Crete, and even Greece. Even when foreign elements such as the Aegean-influenced sacred pillars at the Tarxien temples are evident, they are absorbed into the Maltese aesthetic.[3] When the colonists from Sicily came to settle on Malta sometime in the sixth millennium B.C., the islands must have seemed a center of calm set in a land and sea dominated by the darker aspects of the Goddess' power: although Malta is composed of sedimentary rock, it lies in an area dotted by volcanoes. The Malta that the settlers encountered was probably more fertile and abundantly vegetated than it is today and, in J. D. Evans' words, "must have provided a nearly perfect setting for a peaceful and industrious people to develop a material culture and civilization all their own."[4] It is a culture that is mysterious in its incongruities: the technical and aesthetic achievement of the megalithic buildings is accentuated by the primitive stone implements the inhabitants used and the evidence that they lived in caves or in huts, not constructed settlements. They appear not to have had weapons, nor did they use metals — whether out of primitivism or religious prohibition is unknown. We know practically nothing about their daily lives or social organization, save what we can glean from the sacred buildings. As Sibylle von Cles-Reden found, their religious observances appear to have occupied all of their creative energies.[5]

And while it is true that, as Gertrude Levy notes, the island's sacred ruins constitute "the most complete surviving expression in stone of Neolithic abstract vision"[6] and that their architectural ancestry can be traced back to the rock-cut tombs of Sardinia, Sicily, and Malta itself, yet there is something remarkably different about the aesthetic that governs in Malta: in the unique combination of the fluid lines of the buildings with their carefully fitted monumental stones, the interplay between the lintel and the building blocks themselves and in the incised curves and spirals. The love of the curved form is everywhere offset by the pervasive sense of mass in architecture and artifact alike; the Maltese Goddess is massive, corpulent, strong. A profound set of beliefs requiring extraordinary human effort as a testament or paean to the Goddess must have underwritten this megalithic achievement. Unlike certain of the Neolithic cultures of Old Europe, where the distinction between the mundane and the sacred was blurred, on these islands the sacral stands apart. The immensity of the task of building is epitomized not only in the labor of the temples but also in the curved walls of the Hal Saflieni Hypogeum, literally wrested from the earth by stone picks. It balances on the fulcrum of a spiritual vision that required monumentality and mass to express the deity's power.

Although we sense Maltese spirituality in these buildings, in the designs incised on them and in the statuary and pottery found within, the precise nature of the ancient belief is hidden from us. The concentrated number of sacred places constructed over roughly one thousand years is tantalizing: Was Malta perhaps an oracular center (as Delphi would be), or a place of pilgrimage? Is it possible to imagine, as did Themistocles Zammit, chief excavator of the ruins, that in these temples were the sites of propitiary rites offered to the dark powers of the sea by seafaring navigators?[7] Are these separate edifices evidence of clans or communities, each of which labored separately at the sacred task? What first inspired humanity to begin the work of building, to move places of worship from the natural caves of the islands to man-made edifices aboveground, while retaining much of the cave-worship architectural vocabulary? Even more thought-provoking is the relationship between places of burial and places of worship, below and above ground, the architectural and decorative details of the one imitating the other.[8]

The earliest sacred place on the islands, Ghar Dalam is a cave sanctuary (*ghar* means "cave" in Maltese). Its ritual use dates back to approximately 5000 B.C., and it served as both a burial place and a place of habitation. It is certainly possible to surmise that its stalactites and stalagmites were worshipped as emblems of the great Goddess of the earth (as they had been for millennia and would continue to be) and that the bones of the dead, stripped of their flesh and dusted with red ocher, were buried in her regenerative womb. It is, though, the rock tombs of Xemxija and Zebbuġ, dating from approximately 4000 B.C., that provide the key to Maltese sacred architecture.

The five tombs at Xemxija, rock-cut by human hands, echo the regenerating womb of the caves and look forward to the great temple architecture. All have the same kidney shape, a sacred form to be found in the temples, with a small circular entrance, or "porthole" as Evans calls it, at the bottom of a shaft. One of the tombs is a double chamber, each with its own entrance but connected by a linking corridor. Each of the tombs has recesses, but most important to the later sacred architecture is the manner in which, in the largest tombs (measuring twenty by eighteen feet), portions of the raw rock were left to support the roof of the excavated cave. The lobed forms of the rock-cut tombs are echoed in the first of the megalithic temples, as they will be throughout sacred Maltese architecture, for reasons of spiritual tradition rather than structure.

The temple of Red Skorba on the island of Malta, begun in the mid-fifth millennium, is one of the oldest sacred edifices, although, like the others that would follow, it was changed and elaborated over the centuries. Located on a hill roughly 375 feet above sea level, half a mile away from where the temple of Mġarr would be built, Skorba was first a settlement, as archaeological evidence shows. The site on the hill, part of a ridge overlooking a valley, was probably chosen for the nearby arable land as well as the proximity of a spring in a neighboring valley to the north. Westward, a mile and a half away, is the sheltered Gnejna Bay. Although we do not know why, the settlement was, to use the excavator's phrase, "redeveloped" as a sacred site, and in order to accommodate the building of the temple, a terrace was built up out of the natural slope to provide a foundation for the building. Excavations revealed that even before the erection of the temple, the mud-hutted village possessed an important shrine, the largest feature of the village; its importance might well have dictated its supersession by the megalithic temple. The main room of the early shrine is oval (the so-called North Room), and was entered at its western end; south of this room was a smaller room in a D shape. Stone-paved courtyards, probably open to the sky, lay to the east and west. Terra-cotta and stone figurines of the Goddess found in the North Room showed figures with schematized breasts (indicated by oblique ridges), large incised pubic triangles, and exaggerated buttocks; the heads of these figurines are cylindrical, the facial features represented by a triangle, like those of the Hamangia and Vinča cultures. Other fragments demonstrate that the depictions of the Goddess often included a necklace as well as a girdle. A cowrie shell, ancient symbol of the Goddess' regenerative vulva, was found in the shrine as well. Shards of pottery and the bones of domestic animals were found in abundance. Sacral symbolism familiar from Sardinia and Sicily seems to hint at rites of regeneration, although the absence of human bones in the sacred precinct suggests that they might not have been connected to funerary rites: six goat skulls with long straight horns as well as ox horns were found in the shrine.

The temple of Red Skorba is a three-lobed structure radiating off a central court entered by a center passage, recalling the shape of the rock-cut tombs. At the inner end of this passage once stood massive orthostats over twelve feet high; a smaller pair stood behind them. What rites can we imagine taking place within the walls of the temple? Six-inch holes in the slabs that form the floor might have been used for libations to the deity; the fact that they impede entering and exiting the passageway points to some ritual use, as does the existence of similar holes at the Ġgantija.[9] Fragments of an ochered stone bowl in the center of the temple suggest a specific ritual area. When Red Skorba was remodeled in the Tarxien phase, rectangular limestone altars were added, one of them entirely covered in red clay, as well as trilithon altars; a plaque incised with the image of a temple facade was found behind an altar. Animal sacrifice was practiced within the temple, as evidence of places to tether the animals tells us. During this same period, a second temple was added to the east of the first, a pattern of expansion that occurs at most of Malta's sacred sites and that, as we will see, may be possessed of symbolic import. Most intriguing at Red Skorba, though, are the two external rooms added to the temple, sometime after its

Ghar Dalam Cave, Malta

The earliest holy place on the islands, perhaps the site of the first collective burials as well as worship, the Ghar Dalam Cave contained shards of storage jars and finer pots, decorated with chevrons, zigzags, and hatched triangles.

completion, on its west side. One of these rooms was circular, with a diameter of ten feet; its walls and its floors had been heavily ochered, leading the excavator to call it the Red Room. The second room, unochered and called the Yellow Room, was oval and lay to the west. Were these special sacral areas, serving specific rites?

Nearby, built in an oval shape and entered through the long side, the temple of Mġarr, dating from 4000 B.C., is divided into three rounded chambers or recesses. This is the pattern, later elaborated, of Maltese sacred architecture: "a group of chambers centering about a central spine composed of courts and corridors." Evans' observation that this pattern is hardly simple for a building in stone, and that indeed it is a reproduction of the rock-cut tomb, provides us with the first hint of the raison d'être for the sacred buildings: that the rituals of Malta grew from a cult of the dead, with a Goddess of regeneration at its center.[10] We are struck that the amount of effort required to build this form somehow reflects upon the relationship between humanity and the Goddess. The lobed structure echoing the body of the Goddess as she is figured in Malta may remind us of the ancient forms of the cave and tombs, but with an all-important difference in use and symbolism: although the temples of Malta are an act of conscious imitation of the body of the Goddess, it is unlikely that they ever served as burial places. As the rites and ritual that dominated Malta gained in complexity, so the sacred precincts required more space, grandeur, and even mass: the first temple at Mġarr measures only thirty-five by twenty-five feet overall, but the second achieved a size of sixty by fifty feet, with more formalized and articulated parts. Megalithic slabs form the facade, the corridors, and the portals, and the temple itself is surrounded by a solid exterior wall.

The island of Gozo, on which the Ġgantija stands, is, the Maltese believe, the island of Calypso in legend, whose association with the Goddess of regeneration as a symbol of eternal life is preserved for us in Homer's *Odyssey*. Two temples, one smaller than the other, stand on the site, surrounded by a megalithic outer wall composed of a series of huge slabs set on end. Was the smaller temple, later in date than the first, built to accommodate an increasingly complex ritual, as Evans speculated? Or, as Gimbutas suggests, is the linkage symbolically important, emblematic of the Goddess in her dual aspects as mother and daughter, death and regeneration, or even maturity and youth? Or, as Levy had it, do the two temples symbolize the Goddess and a young "Dying God" consort?[11] The precise meaning of the configuration eludes us, but the symbolism of two temples linked as a unit begins at Red Skorba and Mġarr and continues throughout Maltese tradition.

The symbolism of the interiors of the Ġgantija is less obscure. In both buildings, the rounded chambers (three in one, two in the other) come off a square inner court; the

The Ġgantija

The ritual architecture of Malta included, from the time of the Ġgantija temples forward, both altars and niches, formed of slabs.

interior walls lean inward and were probably covered with timber or stone slabs. Mortar smoothed the rough edges of the different-size rocks that formed the walls, and they were painted red, as traces of color show. Slabs formed niches as well as "altars" set in the passage leading from the inner to the outer chamber. In the larger temple's eastern apse, a shallow stone basin more than three feet in diameter may have served as a ritual hearth; a pillar in this apse has a carving of a snake rising upward, another symbol of the Goddess' regenerative power. The center apse contained a triple shrine. What took place in the Ġgantija's inner chambers can only be guessed at, but surely the ritual, ringed with the reflection of red from the walls in the light cast by hand-held lamps, concerned the eternal cycle of life and death symbolized in and controlled by the Goddess. The enclosed round space of the Ġgantija must have felt like both a womb and a tomb, all-enveloping, dwarfing the humans within it, part of the earth yet rising out of it. As Vincent Scully points out, entering this temple (and the others) would have meant "a return to the goddess and issuing forth a kind of renewal or rebirth."[12] It is tantalizing to think that perhaps the earth itself holds the secret to the rites of the Ġgantija: an eighteenth-century antiquarian claimed that he discovered a labyrinth of tombs beneath the temple itself, which has, as of yet, never been rediscovered. If the labyrinth exists, as von Cles-Reden points out, it is possible that the shrine on the surface, the Ġgantija, "may have been only the entrance to a still bigger shrine beneath."[13]

What makes that incredible idea even thinkable is the mysterious and compelling structure on Malta known as the Hal Saflieni Hypogeum, a rock-cut city of the dead, begun in the fourth millennium, comprising three stories, the lowest of which (and the latest in date) reaches a depth of thirty feet below the surface of the hill into which it was cut. These catacombs were dug over a period of hundreds of years; picks of horn and stone mallets were used to excavate and shape the soft limestone, while smoothing was done with small flint blades. The care and effort of creation is amazing. Over the course of roughly eleven hundred years, the bones of some seven thousand people were interred here, along with funeral goods of necklaces and pottery as well as polished green axes too blunt to be used as weapons, perhaps symbols of sacrifice or regeneration. The ancient practice of burial with red ocher continued; when the Hypogeum was excavated and water from a modern structure above spilled into the sanctuary, the bones seemed afloat in a sea of blood. The megalithic structure, perhaps a temple, that once stood above the Hypogeum has vanished, and modern buildings constructed above the site have damaged the original entrance, yet the structure carved into the earth has lost none of its mystery. The first level of cells is irregular in shape and roughly finished, but the lines of the rest of the Hypogeum are curved and concave, with rounded vaults. As the second level reveals, it probably served as both a catacomb and a holy place for rite and ritual. The burial cells of the upper level yield to long vaulted halls, painted with red ocher in patterns of spirals, honeycombs, and dots and circles. One ceiling has a black-and-white checkerboard pattern. On this level of the Hypogeum the limestone again becomes a surface to embellish and on which to imitate the masonry of the island's later temples: one hall has an elaborate megalithic facade carved into one end, with corbeled blocks set above. The continuing reflexive relationship between burial places below ground and the sacred edifices above blurs the distinction between the veneration of the dead and the ways (and place) of the worship of the living, a relationship hinted at in the tombs of Sardinia and Sicily but here made explicit. The deliberate repetition and exchange of details illumines a key aspect of the spirituality of Malta: the circularity, the connectiveness, between life and death reinforced again and again. As Gertrude Levy noted, "Here the sacred character of a familiar temple construction is artificially imposed to intensify the sanctity of the cave, just as cave sanctity is invoked by the structural forms above ground."[14] That the Goddess of Malta reigns in both places is shown by the artifice of humanity.

Small chambers open up off the first hall of the Hypogeum's upper level, each with a miniature trilithon entrance, two uprights with a horizontal slab above both. A door in the middle of the carved facade yields to another elaborately carved chamber, and behind it lies a kidney-shaped room reminiscent of the tombs at Xemxija in which secret rites were perhaps performed. There is archaeological evidence that these rites were intended to be kept secret even from those who were permitted within the labyrinth's precincts; possibly the rites were the sole domain of priestesses or priests. What privileged few were permitted to enter — and why — is, of course, unknown to us, but it seems likely that the Hypogeum was never a place for public worship, although the structure that once surmounted it may well have been.

The Hypogeum must have been a spectral place, with dim light thrown from burning fat (there is no evidence of the blackening that would have accompanied the use of torches) flickering over the curved walls, disappearing into the deep shadows of the niches. The carvings as well as the red ocher decorations would have been visible one moment and invisible the next. Descending into the Hypogeum out of the brightness and heat of the sun must have also intensified the effect of this cool and dark city of the dead, an effect present in the temples above the ground as well. The curved lines of the dark walls must have clasped the visitor to the earth, source of life and the land of the dead. Was it the embrace of the earth or the spirits of the dead that empowered the Hypogeum as a sanctuary, a place for the practice of dream incubation, divination, and perhaps a cult of healing?

Hal Saflieni Hypogeum: "The Holy of the Holies"

The red ocher that once stained these walls has left no trace, but it is not difficult to recover the spectral sense of awe these chambers must have inspired. The elements that imitate the above-ground sacred architecture flicker in and out of view, insisting with each reappearance on the holiness of the place, the inner earth transformed by humanity in the Goddess' name.

One hall of the Hypogeum is surrounded by small cells, which were probably used for dream incubation, the practice of sleeping within a holy place in order to gain access to its power through revelatory and prophetic dreams. Two statuettes of sleeping figures, one exquisitely modeled, hint at the existence of oracular priestesses within the Hypogeum's depths. Off the left side of the oblong chamber lies the Oracle Room, its highly arched ceiling decorated with an elaborate red scroll pattern, suggestive of both the tree of life and the regenerative power of nature.[15] The Oracle Room has a recess with extraordinary acoustics: a voice speaking in it resonates throughout the vaults; this is probably where the oracular directives were spoken. The presence of similar apertures with the same acoustical properties in side chambers at the temples of Mnajdra, Ħaġar Qim, and Tarxien indicates that some form of communication with the spiritual world (emissaries of the dead, or perhaps the Goddess herself?) was a part of Maltese rite. The ancient belief in the power of a sacred site to convey oracular messages is preserved not only in the later Greek tradition (as at Delphi) but also in the Homeric epics' description of the gods and the goddesses' ability to communicate to humans in the form of dreams. Marija Gimbutas posits that these rooms may have been used for rites of initiation (for "to sleep within the Goddess' womb was to die and to come to life anew") and that the statuettes could be votive offerings from those who had successfully passed through the rites. The presence of a statuette of a sleeping fish, formerly a source of confusion and mystery to commentators, has been explained by Gimbutas as a symbol of the Goddess in her regenerative aspect in Old Europe (as it is on the Cycladic "frying pans"), thus supporting the theories of both dream incubation and initiation.[16] The presence of figures with oddly distended body parts, some pierced with shells, and sculptures of body parts suggest too that the site was connected to a cult of healing; the connection between oracular sites and healing cults occurs again historically in Greece, at the Temple of Asepius at Epidaurus.

Another testament to the Hypogeum's function as a place for the rites of the living is the room known as the Holy of the Holies. Once again, the below-ground chamber has been carved to imitate the facade of a domed building, with a deeply curved wall broken by a doorway in the middle and shallow niches on either side. Two conical pits sealed with plugs pierce the floor on the left of the door. Within one of them, excavators found a pair of sheep's horns, perhaps either a symbol of regeneration or the remains of a sacrifice to the Goddess.

The Hypogeum was begun at approximately the same time as the Ġgantija, but was continued during the successive periods that saw the building of the other great temple complexes on the islands: Ħaġar Qim, Mnajdra, and Tarxien.

Sleeping Goddess (4000 B.C.)

The curves of her body are lush and rounded, femaleness in full flower; the room she was found in was egg-shaped, as are her buttocks, symbol of regenerative power. Traces of pigment remind us that this clay sculpture was once painted red, the color of life; the chambers of the Hypogeum too were awash with red. She is asleep in a place of the dead, which is also the regenerative womb of the Goddess. Did her dream-filled sleep yield the voice of prophecy, or did she communicate with the spirits of the dead? We will never know with certainty whether she is the Goddess herself or a priestess; in either guise she radiates calm.

**Limestone Figurine
from Ħaġar Qim Temple**

The power of the female
expressed in volume and
lush curves.

96

Near the village of Qrendi lie the ruins of the complex known as Ħaġar Qim, overlooking the south coast of Malta and the luminous sea beyond. The site must have long been sacred since smaller shrines existed here before the megalithic monuments. Ħaġar Qim, a mass of additions and rebuilding, is made entirely of globigerina limestone, giving it a golden glow. Although the soft stone weathers badly, it is also easy to work, and at Ħaġar Qim the full possibilities of the Maltese aesthetic were explored, for it is rich in exquisite, symbolic decoration. That this is a precinct of the Goddess is evident from the images and symbols inscribed in stone: here we find the sacred snake topped by a triangle on an altar and sacred plant forms emblematic of regeneration. The facade of the building was built of massive slabs that must have once stood thirty or forty feet high. Behind it lies a series of chambers in the shape and configuration of the traditional ovals. The temple also has the stone recesses seen at the Ġgantija; in smaller ones, some fitted with covers, the bones of small animals were found, presumably sacrificed within the sacred precincts. Carved altars with plant motifs, still bearing traces of the red paint that once covered them, also bear witness to the rites that once took place here.

A few hundred yards below the ruins of Hagar Qim lie those of Mnajdra. Nestled in a hollow with a view of the sea are double temples, side by side, one smaller than the other as at the Ġgantija; both have two sets of lateral chambers and a small rear recess behind the second pair. The southwest building was probably the older one, with walls made of huge, dressed slabs. Steps lead to an opening in one of the slabs, which yields to a small chamber between the back of the inner wall and the outer casing of the temple; niches here, some with elaborately carved pillars and others without, suggest ritual significance. Was it a shrine, or a place to store ritual objects? The second temple also has a wall slab pierced in the same way, although no evidence of a chamber survives. What does survive, though, is a small room behind the walls of the southwest chamber: a slab framed by a trilithon contains a windowlike opening leading to a tiny chamber. Within the chamber is a small niche made up of slabs with a central pillar. The entrance to the first temple is decorated all over with pocking, producing a honeycomb effect; Marija Gimbutas suggests that these markings may be like the cupmark, a sign that invoked the Goddess from La Ferrassie to sacred sites in Ireland, and constitute a "penetration into her element."[17]

The Cordin plateau, site of both the Tarxien temples and the Hypogeum (and perhaps its long-lost megalithic temple), appears to have been both a center of human activity and an extremely holy place. The buildings must have been visible for miles; indeed, Ħaġar Qim to the southwest would have been visible to worshippers at Tarxien.[18] There are three separate sanctuaries at Tarxien. In the main court of the third temple stood a colossal statue, over eight feet high, of a female figure, perhaps the Maltese Goddess herself. Her shape, her details, her mass are consistent with small figurines found elsewhere. Symbols of regenerative power abound at Tarxien: in addition to female figurines (most of which have marked pubes) and stone triangles (some with holes, perhaps indicating the vulva) are phalluses, as well as an incised relief of two horned bulls, one of which stands above a sow with thirteen suckling piglets. A snake's head made out of a stalactite was found here, and snakes were scratched onto potsherds. The stone altars at Tarxien show evidence of animal sacrifice — indeed, one altar slab is decorated with a frieze of sheep, a pig, and a ram, presumably all sacrificial animals — as well as evidence of burned sacrifices. Shells too were apparently offered in sacrifice, for they were found in heaps near the fireplaces; clay models of shells found at Tarxien and at Mnajdra attest to their sacral symbolism. In the ruins too were many pillars, symbols of the Goddess and her presence, an incorporation of Aegean practices into Maltese ritual.

We will never know precisely what the ancient worship of Malta entailed, nor can we confirm with any certainty the spiritual sense that impelled the building of these great monuments. The scale of the buildings and that of the statue at Tarxien seem to proclaim the awesome power of the Maltese deity, and the corresponding diminution of human proportions. Were the Maltese protected by the arc of the giant Goddess' skirt, or did they stand trembling in the shadow it cast over them? The shape of the temples echoing the volume of the Goddess' body, the red walls emblematic of the blood of life, the decorative symbols of fruition, and the oracle holes suggest the former: that the gulf between deity and humanity could be bridged. The practice of sacrifice also suggests that the Goddess' mighty chthonic power could be propitiated and assuaged. The free exchange of architectural vocabularies and details between the places of the dead and those of the living is an eloquent testimony to the circularity of the life cycle, as is the continuous task of building, rebuilding, and creating.

The civilization of Malta ends abruptly. The archaeological evidence shows no decline or change but, simply, an ending. Zammit speculated that a plague had destroyed the island's population, but others believe that the temple folk were exterminated by armed invaders from across the sea.[19] These intruders, named the Tarxien Cemetery people (for where their remains were found), used copper axes and daggers and adorned themselves with jewelry made of blue faience. They too worshipped a goddess, about whom we know little save that she was depicted in schematic form, decorated with geometric patterns, seated on a throne. Unlike their predecessors, the Cemetery people cremated their dead. The inspired aesthetic of Malta was replaced by crude pottery and rough dolmens. The unmaintained temples began to crumble but still, as D. H. Trump points out, must have remained awe-inspiring, even to subsequent invaders, for the Tarxien Cemetery people were themselves overrun.[20]

Tarxien Temples, Malta

According to David Trump, the facade of these temples might once have risen thirty feet in the air and spanned more than one hundred feet.

Perhaps what we should retain in our imaginations of the old Malta is the vision of how the temples looked, both to the islands' inhabitants as they gazed out toward the sea and to mariners as they looked landward: the huge gray and yellow stones shining in the sunlight, perched atop the small outcroppings of land in the midst of the Mediterranean, evidence of both human diligence and the Goddess' power. Perhaps here in these sacred precincts, as Zammit imagined, mariners and other pilgrims gave themselves over to the Maltese Goddess. Finally, it is the beauty, created in the service of the Goddess, that stays with us longest: the fine lines of the carving, the modeling of the figurines, the permanence of the worked-over stones.

RIGHT: **Goddess from Haġar Qim Temple**

The womanly and maternal curves of this five-inch terra-cotta figurine remind us of the Goddess of the Paleolithic and the centrality of the female form to the Maltese religious vision.

LEFT: **Goddess from Tarxien Temples**

Only the right-hand lower portion of this colossal statue remains, but once this figure of the Goddess stood roughly eight feet high.

OVERLEAF: **Malta at Night**

Paired Menhirs,
Finistère, Brittany

6 Sacred Stones

In France and England the earth rises up into artificial rectangular hillocks, long since overgrown by vegetation; beneath these barrows lie ancient places of worship and burial, covered by rocky layers of dirt. Inland from the coasts of England, petrified shapes rise up out of the often misty chalky plains. At Carnac in Brittany, three thousand stones cluster in a five-mile area. An enormous regiment of 1099 menhirs, arranged in parallel rows, advance toward a semicircle of seventy slabs, ranging in size from barely two feet tall to twelve feet high as they near the sacred precinct. The green of Ireland is scattered with stone circles and burial mounds, some of them carved and embellished with the iconographic signs of the Goddess, perhaps created by settlers from other places who brought their sacred rites with them. These places are all sacred precincts, originally set off from the hills and plains. Monumental sacred stones, memories of an ancient past, stand bent, overgrown by peat and moss, changed by wind and time. And yet they are not voiceless.

It is their grandeur first that strikes us: implacable slabs of stone that seem to grow upright out of the body of the earth, as if they were hewn against the sky. As the mind takes in their majesty and mystery, it recognizes too the immensity of the human effort required to build them: the dirt and stones piled for the barrows, the many miles of menhirs lifted onto the land of Brittany, the careful dressing of the stones at Stonehenge. The tremendous weight and size of the stones makes their scale seem beyond human capability. It is no wonder that many of them — like the Roche aux Fées (the Rock of the Fairies) in France — were thought by the generations that followed to have been built by supernatural beings or giants.

These monuments are diverse. They are the products of different cultures, located on various terrains and perhaps even serving different purposes, but they share an underlying common thread: the stone itself. Stone is the great symbol of permanence that, early in human history, came to stand for the eternal and the divine.[1] Its massiveness could protect the dead and stand as a bulwark against transience; its seeming imperviousness to the elements made it a symbol of the imperishable. An offspring of the earth, of the Goddess' body, stone took on some of her supernatural aspects, magical and mysterious. Long after the ancient rites had been forgotten, the power of the stones remained intact in folklore and legend; as recently as the early years of this century, Breton couples hoping to conceive went to the menhirs for aid.[2] It was said too that ancestral spirits hovered not only in the Breton *allées* but around the stone circles of England and Ireland.

OPPOSITE PAGE:
The Menhirs of Carnac

Carnac

Sibylle von Cles-Reden reminds us that the Gauls called Brittany "the land on the sea" and that the sea dominates Brittany's existence. The menhirs (from the Welsh *maen* for "stone" and *hir* for "long") that march in formation at Carnac were long believed by the local people to have mysterious powers, a trace memory perhaps of the sacred rites in which these stones once played a part. Marija Gimbutas stresses that the menhir is an epiphany of the Owl Goddess, whose features are sometimes inscribed on standing stones in France, Spain, and Portugal. These menhirs form a part of what once was a sacred precinct: elongated mounds — as much as three hundred feet long, one hundred feet wide, and thirty-six feet high — also dot the land around Carnac, holding within them stone chambers of the dead, in which the bodies had been partly burnt. Among the goods found in these passage graves were unused and, in Glyn Daniel's words, "superbly made" axes of fibrolite and greenstone, as well as double axes of stone.

And yet, while the stones are of the earth, human labor in honor of a greater power is everywhere evident in their placement and construction.

Like the sacred sites of Malta, the stone megaliths that dot the British Isles and Ireland represent work that spanned generations. Quantifying the work of the megalith builders in England will give a practical dimension to their spiritual devotion and effort. It has been calculated that the ditch and bank at Avebury took some 1.5 million hours of work. The strength of more than two hundred people was needed to move and place a single block of the gigantic entrance. The great mound of Silbury, not stone but a carefully constructed artificial earthen tumulus, rises 138 feet in the air and is 550 feet in diameter. It can be seen from the Avebury henges and is part of their sacred precinct. Roughly 12.5 million cubic feet of earth were moved to raise it; it has been estimated that it took some 18 million hours of labor to complete.[3] Stonehenge was first constructed around 3000 B.C. and was rebuilt and elaborated some twelve hundred years later; its massive plinths rise sixty feet in the air and weigh many hundreds of tons. As Aubrey Burl has pointed out,

LEFT: **The Goddess of Grimes Grave** (c. 2850 B.C.)

According to Marija Gimbutas, figurines of the Goddess, as well as other artifacts, were found in the copper mines of Old Europe, linking that tradition to this figure found in a flint mine in Norfolk, England, and suggesting a connection between the Goddess and the fruits of the earth, metal and flint.

ABOVE: **West Kennet Barrow, Part of the Sacred Precinct of Avebury**

the building of Stonehenge was "a marvel of design and administration that demanded the labours of hundreds, perhaps thousands, over many years." Burl's vivid reconstruction of the final elaboration of Stonehenge both thrills and strains the modern imagination:

> From the Marlborough Downs seventy-seven sarsens were achingly hauled, each an average of twenty-six dragging tons, over grass, stream, downslope, long pulls around the Pewsey marshes, up the inch-inch-inch backstraining steepiness of Redborn Hill, and more miles across the West Down, ropes greasy-black with sweat, day by day, to the last exhausted exultant sight of the Heel Stone, two months of strain for a thousand or more people, fed by others, the settlements for miles empty of all but the old. One stone a year may have been all.[4]

The act of building the sacred precinct itself takes on the form of ritual, as does the demanding labor. The West Kennet barrow, part of the sacred precinct of Avebury, is 320 to 340 feet long, while the burial chamber itself occupies only 45 feet. Was the size of the monument ritually important? Was communal labor part of the ritual? The structures, too, take on another dimension when we imagine the tools that were probably wielded by those who dug Stonehenge's ditch and built Silbury Hill: picks made of antler, shovels of the shoulder blade of an ox, woven wicker baskets to hold tools and debris.[5]

Surely the immensity of the human effort reflects the belief underlying rite, although the precise meanings and objects of devotion remain veiled. In England, unlike Ireland and the Continent, precious few artifacts or symbolic carvings attesting to the nature of religious belief survive. The single chalk figure of a Pregnant Goddess tantalizes us with her possible secrets: she was found, along with a realistically carved phallus, at the bottom of an apparently unproductive flint mine at Grimes Grave in Norfolk. Flints were heaped at her feet, with seven red deer antlers laid close by, presumably part of a supplication to the mined earth to renew its riches. Amid the antlers were carved balls of chalk. Balls made of chalk were found not only in graves at Windmill Hill but at New Grange in Ireland, where the megalithic stones are incised with concentric circles; in the ditch at Stonehenge; and buried with the body of a young woman at Avebury.[6] Also found at Stonehenge were two decorated chalk plaques, one with a pattern of right-angled zigzags filled in with dots and cross-hatching; on the reverse side are lozenges. The second plaque is filled with chevrons and a lozenge.[7] Without denying the differences that separate Neolithic England from the mainland of Europe, it is difficult not to see the iconography of the Goddess of death and regeneration as she was realized elsewhere. The generative power of the Goddess is schematically expressed by triangles and lozenges; the aquatic symbols of the Goddess are zigzags, multiple arcs, and cupmarks.[8] It is worth noting that many of the stone henges and circles of the late Neolithic are located near water.

The Folkton Drums too make us strain over the plains and valleys of the English horizon for a clearer view of the Goddess. The drums are small cylindrical objects found in a rounded barrow in Yorkshire that covered a cairn of flint, chalk, and stone in which two adults had been buried. Two ditches encircled the barrow, and on the inner edge of the outer ditch, an oval pit had been dug. The pit contained the body of a five-year-old child, her hands in front of her face. Beneath her head lay a chalk drum beautifully carved with a design of chevrons and triangles, and marked with an incised eye; cross-hatching and herringbone patterns also appear. Beneath the hips of the child were two other cylinders, with grooved circles on their tops, more triangles, net and chevron patterns, and eyes and eyebrows — designs emblematic of the Neolithic Goddess. Marija Gimbutas identifies the drum shape with the Bird Goddess and sees the eyes on the drums as the Owl Goddess, Goddess of death.[9] It is possible too that the other patterns represent the Goddess in her other aspects, including life-giver and regeneratrix. The placement of the child among these symbolic objects of the Goddess' power resonates with meaning: the girl may have been a sacrificial offering, thus empowering the ring that enclosed the burial precinct.[10]

The only other English artifact that appears to hold ritual significance is the ax, symbol of the Goddess elsewhere, in Brittany and the Aegean. The axes, concealed in the henges and earthworks of England, at Llandegai, Cairnapple, Mount Pleasant, and Stonehenge, as well as apparently ritual clay axes found in the pits of Stonehenge and Woodhenge, indicate the Goddess' presence in the English countryside. A tiny polished ax was found in Devon at Kingwear, while unused bronze axes were buried with the dead in Yorkshire. Axes are also carved into the stone of the sarsens at Stonehenge.

But it is to the carved menhirs of Brittany and to the more than nine hundred stone circles of England, Ireland, Scotland, and the other sacred precincts that we must finally turn to find the presence of the Goddess and the rites that honored her.

Sometime around 4500 B.C. the British Isles were settled by farmers, and one of the earliest known barrows (that of Lambourne in Berkshire) dates from about 250 years later, providing the first glimpse of the outlines of rite and religion. These barrows, made of a spine of sarsen boulders, were mounded with chalk rubble and dirt and topped with turf; skeletons were buried at the east end. These were probably sites common to a single family; bones already stripped of their flesh were brought to wooden mortuary huts, the entrances of which were oriented toward the rising moon, or to the sunrise. From another barrow, that of Fussell's Lodge, we may surmise that bodies were first cremated and then the cleansed bones carried to the mortuary where they would be ritually handled in ceremony. This pattern of rite would stay constant in England for the next few thousand years, as would the solar and lunar orientation of the sacred precincts. The barrows, though they may have begun as burial places, became centers for rites, possibly involving communion with the dead or invocation of the chthonic spirit of the earth.[11] Human sacrifices, as acts of propitiation, may have been included. There is continuity as well in the precincts themselves: Avebury henge is surrounded by barrows, as is Stonehenge, where fifteen barrows lie within three miles.

It is the passage graves of New Grange, Dowth, and Knowth in Ireland, built roughly a thousand years after the first barrows, that lead toward the heart of the religion of the Goddess in the British Isles. The area near a bend in the river Boyne was once considered holy to its people, as evidenced by New Grange and by its neighboring mounds at Dowth and Knowth, and by the extraordinary number of earthworks (some forty, bordered on three sides by the river) in the surrounding area, some of which were once surrounded by standing stones. The tomb of New Grange rises some 45 feet in height and is 265 feet in diameter. It has been reconstructed, in modern times, and its top is now covered with grass, blending in with its surroundings, but originally New Grange had symbolic prominence in the landscape. Rising to an even greater height than it does today,

The Folkton Drums
(c. 2000 B.C.)

it was probably entirely covered with white stones, with a single megalith rising from its top. The mound was built without a ditch or a bank, and the bottom was marked by curbstones, only some of which have survived but which may have numbered as many as one hundred. Possibly half of these stone slabs were decorated with symbols of the Goddess, spirals and lozenges among them.[12] The mound itself was once circled by thirty-five menhirs, of which twelve still survive, that separated the sacred place from its profane surroundings.

This once holy place is oriented toward the midwinter's sunrise; in fact, it has been suggested that its name derives from *an uamh greine*, or "cave of the sun."[13] In the southeast quadrant of the circular mound, leading in from a richly decorated curbstone, is a sixty-two-foot passage that yields to a central chamber, out of which open three chambers. Originally the entrance to the passage would have been blocked by earth and stones; within, the connection between the passage and the central chamber would have been closed by a massive stone. The passageway is walled with big stone slabs, twenty-one on the right side and twenty-two on the left, of which thirteen are decorated. The passageway is narrow (three feet wide), and its height, culminating in a corbeled roof, rises and falls intermittently from below five feet to slightly above seven, a fact that would have required crawling at least part of the way to reach the inner chamber. This central chamber, about ten feet across, rises to a height of just under twenty feet. Two of the three adjacent chambers contained large stone basins, the largest three and a half by six feet long, the smallest three and a half by four feet. In the right chamber, the basins were stacked, one above the other.

We are in the presence of the Goddess, in her sanctuary, signaled by the intricacy of the pecked-out designs on the stones. The Goddess at the tomb of New Grange is seen in her aspects of the owl and the snake, symbolizing both death and regeneration. The curbstone at the entrance to the burial chamber is incised with double and triple spirals as well as lozenges; the spirals, symbols of the Goddess as the source of life energy, are in triple form, that energy at "its most potent."[14] The lozenge too signifies her power of regeneration, as do the halved lozenges, sacred triangles, that decorate the narrow false lintel which once stood above the entrance. The corbel in the south side chamber, decorated with lozenges and zigzags, evokes water, aspect of the Goddess as life-giver, as do the cupmarks on a curbstone and on the stone slabs of the passageway. The underside of the capstone of the eastern chamber has the eyes and beak of the Owl Goddess of death, combined with symbols of energy (snake coils) flanked by signs of life (the aquatic zigzag) and interspersed with V-shapes, chevrons, lozenges, zigzags, and winding serpents.[15] These designs had a ritual purpose hidden from humanity's view — perhaps that of

New Grange
The passageway and the corbeled roof, as seen from inside the chamber.

invocation of the Goddess into the sacred precinct — as demonstrated by the pattern of pocked lozenges and triangles, the vulva of rebirth, on the underside of a corbel stone, concealed when New Grange was in use but now visible because another slab has fallen forward.[16]

New Grange was both a house for the dead and a place of rebirth. As the iconography of its art encompasses life, death, and regeneration, so does its spatial orientation and superstructure (a roof box above the entrance to the tomb). The passage to the tomb is aligned with the path where the sun of the midwinter solstice would rise; even with the entrance to the tomb blocked by earth and stone, when the two quartz slabs were pushed aside the rectangular opening above the entrance would admit the rays of the sun. Out of the darkness of midwinter, the passageway and even the innermost recesses of the chambers and the bones of the dead laid there would be illuminated; the triple spiral of the Goddess would be suffused with life-giving radiance. What role the stone basins in the side chambers may have played in the rites of rebirth is unclear but the presence of grave goods and cremated bones hints at a performed ceremony, perhaps involving rebirth. The elaborate effort made to keep the spirits of the dead dry and comfortable has been noted by Michael O'Kelly; as he puts it, "The House for the Dead had to be built of great stones so that it should last forever; the houses of the builders themselves must have been ephemeral things of wood and thatch that have disappeared without leaving any trace above ground."[17] Certainly New Grange, located close to water (the river Boyne) and decorated with aquatic signs, suggests that sunlight *and* water might have been part of the symbolic rebirth there.

The tomb of Dowth is roughly the same size as New Grange; it too is surrounded by curbstones though it lacks a circle of freestanding stones. It too has a passageway leading to a central chamber with three side chambers; at Dowth, though, the south chamber has an extension that leads to a rectangular room, the floor of which is a single eight-foot-long stone with an oval hollow at its center. One of the curbstones is decorated with a pattern of rayed suns; within the central chamber, the same pattern appears. Elsewhere, the symbolic patterns, though not as elaborate as those at New Grange, declare the Goddess' presence: concentric circles, zigzags, chevrons, spirals. When Dowth was excavated, balls (like those found in England) as well as fragments of human skulls were discovered within the material of the cairn. Heaps of bones and fragments of burned human bones were found within the chamber, as were the bones of horses, pigs, deer, and birds; beads, bracelets, and copper pins may have been funeral goods or offerings.[18]

The great tomb of Knowth is surrounded by seventeen smaller tombs, many of which are nonetheless substantial in size, and forms a part of the sacred area that includes

BELOW: **New Grange**

The presence of the Goddess
was indicated and embodied
in the carvings. These are
from the west recess; the
third spiral can be seen at
the bottom of the photograph.

ABOVE: **Engraved Stone
Slab, Les Pierres Plates,
Locmariaquer, Brittany**
(c. 3000 B.C.)

In this photograph, the
regenerative vulva of the
Goddess, carved on a slab in
a megalithic tomb, is clearly
visible; the top of the stone
shows the beak and eyebrows
Marija Gimbutas has identified with the Owl Goddess.

LEFT: **The Triple Spiral of
the Goddess at New Grange**

In Marija Gimbutas' words:
"She is one, She is two,
She is three — the totality."

New Grange and Dowth as well as other passage tombs. There may, in fact, have been two or three more tombs than now exist.[19] The vista from the great mound at Knowth would have included an expanse of fertile land — then as now, some of the best farming land in all of Ireland — as well as the neighboring monuments. The center mound of Knowth contained two tombs built back to back, one which opens east and the other west. The corbel-roofed eastern tomb is cruciform in shape with three recesses opening out from its central area. As at New Grange, a highly decorated basin was found in one recess; four feet in diameter, it had been worked by all-over pocking, with three concentric circles flanked by two arcs and a circle above. Near the basin was evidence of cremation. Behind it, in the recess, stood a highly decorated orthostat.

Unlike the tomb at New Grange, the tombs at Knowth orient northeast and southwest, and it has been suggested by George Eògan, the site's excavator, that ceremonial moments in the year could have been celebrated at the mound, one at the vernal equinox and another at the autumnal one, the rebirth of the growing season and the moment of harvest. He suggests too that the back-to-back tombs contained within the mound indicate that rites may have taken place on the east side in the morning and on the west in the evening.[20] Were there open-air ceremonies, a procession around the smaller mounds and then around the central one? Was the central tomb entered on these days by priestesses or priests for communication, perhaps oracular, with the Goddess herself, source of life and death, mother of the seed and of harvest? Did the surrounding tombs play a role in these rites, or did they simply demarcate the sanctified area?

The details are lost to us, but we may surmise that the decorated curbstones here, as at New Grange, would have invoked the Goddess with her sacred signs. Like the other sites, Knowth was decorated with the signs of the Goddess — zigzags, lozenges, pocked surfaces — and while most of the art was meant to be seen, here too is hidden invocatory art, what Gimbutas has called "ritual actions for communication with the divine, an evocation of the Goddess's regenerative powers hidden in stone."[21]

The stone carvings of Ireland, like those of Brittany, reveal the Goddess' presence and illuminate the religion of the builders of the Neolithic great mounds. But the sacred precincts of England — primarily those of Stonehenge, Avebury, and Silbury — reveal the Goddess in another light.

New Grange

The east recess of New Grange, with the sacral basins, both chiseled all over. The upper basin has two circular depressions, side by side. The support behind the basins is a modern addition and part of the New Grange reconstruction. The stone roof above is decorated with the sacred signs of the Goddess.

On a slight rise on the chalk downs of the Salisbury Plains stands Stonehenge. The ruins of this great stone circle are all that is left of a sacred site that was built and elaborated on over the course of several thousand years. We do not know whether this temple — and surely it was a place of rite and ritual — was changed and rebuilt to accommodate new rites or to reflect changes in the religious vision of its people. Stonehenge I, built around 2800 B.C., was primarily an earthworks, a bank in the form of a true circle with a diameter of 320 feet, surrounded by a ditch. The bank has long since been lowered by weather and time, but it once might have been as high as six feet. Within the inner margin of the bank, set in a circular pattern 288 feet in diameter, were the so-called Aubrey holes, named after their seventeenth-century discoverer, John Aubrey. These steep-sided and flat-bottomed pits range from two feet in depth to slightly less than four feet; their width varies from two and a half feet across to over six feet. Outside the entrance to the earthworks, within the Avenue (the processional road), stood two sarsen stones, one of which, the Heel Stone, survives, although the ravages of time and weather have caused it to slope rather than stand upright. The untooled eight-foot-thick Heel Stone rises sixteen feet in the air; four feet of stabilizing stone lie buried in the ground. At the center of the earthen circle, it is thought, stood a wooden building, a ritual edifice which was perhaps gated and roofed, although time and careless digs at the site have obliterated any trace of it.[22]

Stonehenge

The sacred circle of stone is not a static entity but one which changes for the beholder depending on the weather and time of day. In the reflection of light the stones take on different colors, giving them a movement and flexibility that belie their height and weight. Distance and proximity, too, change the vision of Stonehenge and its sacred stones. The monument beckons from afar and then arcs over humanity within the circle of mighty sarsen trilithons. (*Sarsen* is simply a corruption of *Saracen,* a name bestowed on the "pagan" stones by pious Christians.)

OVERLEAF: **Stonehenge**

Avebury Stone Circle

The earthworks itself defined a sacred area, set off symbolically and physically from the surrounding plain, excluding and enclosing at once. What rites were practiced at Stonehenge in its earliest history can be deduced from the solar and lunar alignments built into the earthworks, and from the Aubrey holes. The Heel Stone and the center of the henge were roughly aligned to the midsummer sunrise. Stonehenge I also had lunar orientation. The specific site for the sacred area was chosen precisely because of its unique latitude: the extreme northern and southern risings and settings of the sun and the moon are at right angles to each other here. Stake holes, which possibly record the midwinter risings of the moon over a period of many years, argue as well for lunar orientation.[23] It seems clear that these alignments with lunar and solar risings have less to do with scientific observation than with ritual. We are reminded of the sun of the winter solstice that penetrates the house of the dead at Knowth; at Stonehenge it is the summer solstice that penetrates the circle, at the sun's full height of life-giving power. The regenerative Goddess is also present at Stonehenge as the moon, symbolizing the "archetypal unity and multiplicity of feminine nature. . . . She was the giver of life, and all that promotes fertility, and at the same time she was the wielder of the destructive powers of nature."[24] The Aubrey holes hint that some of the rites concerned propitiation of both the chthonic and regenerative powers. Dug out of the chalky earth, the holes were refilled with the same rubble dug out from them, some of it burned, with charred bits of wood and cremated human bones. One of the pits contained a ritual clay ax, while red clay — reminiscent of the ancient use of red ocher — was found in others. Unburned animal bones, fire-marked antlers, and a chalk bone were also part of the deposits. Richard Atkinson imagines that the pits were connected to rites opening a symbolic door to the netherworld, to the chthonic powers, and to the spirits of the dead, as they were much later in ancient Greece.[25] That these were indeed "dedications to the generative power of the earth" may be substantiated by similar practices at Maumsbury Rings, where the tapering pits plunged as deep as thirty-five feet into the earth, and where they were partly filled with similar offerings, some of them burnt.[26]

The rebuilding of Stonehenge in approximately 2200 B.C. both solidifies and changes the older tradition. A double circle of eighty-two bluestones (so called because of the blue tint they acquire when wet) was added to the center of the earthworks, further delineating the inner heart of the sacred enclosure. These stones, transported from Prescelly on the south coast of Wales, may have been chosen because they came from a sacred mountain. Importantly, the Avenue was now linked to the river Avon, strengthening the connection between the site and water. The solar orientation of the entrance was reemphasized by additional stones, a fact that has prompted some scholars to propose a shift from the earth-centered religious focus to a sky-centered one, from Goddess to gods.[27] Yet the lunar orientations of the temple were not destroyed and the symbolic connection to water was strengthened, suggesting that a ritual similiar to a sacred marriage — of male and female elements, both sun and moon — might have begun to dominate the rites at Stonehenge. Could it be that "the sun and the moon were parts of the cosmology of people who still looked to the earth for protection, handling the dead bones and the skulls of ancestors in the warm days of summer and the frozen nights of winter"?[28]

The final phase of the rebuilding of Stonehenge, which probably took place over three distinct periods, further obscures our vision of rite and ritual. For unknown reasons, this rebuilding, sometime in the first millennium, was never completed, but through its successive stages openness is banished: the bluestones were first replaced by a circle of massive sarsens in the same position and alignment, topped by stone lintels. Within the great sarsen circle stood five sarsen trilithons, arranged in a horseshoe shape, open toward the northeast. Most thought-provoking is the way that the construction of the trilithons imitates carpentry: carefully wrought tenons and mortises connect the lintels to the uprights. Is this simulation in stone a symbolic evocation of earlier places of worship wrought in timber, a way of integrating past and present, new rites and old, as it was in Malta? The sight of the great stone circle with its thirty trilithons — the uprights rising to

123

almost fourteen feet, its lintels over ten feet long — must have been awe-inspiring. Stonehenge grew ever more complex: a circle of bluestones was added between the sarsen circle and the horseshoe, and then the horseshoe itself was filled with an oval of monumental bluestones. The Four Stations Stone and the so-called Slaughter Stone and its companion were added. It seems likely that the older communal ceremonies gave way to rites performed by a few; there is evidence that the orientation of the temple became turned toward the midwinter sunset, perhaps an indication that the very basis for rite had shifted.[29] We will probably never know what prompted this stage of Stonehenge, but we may look to a neighboring sacred precinct, that of Avebury, for another vision of the Goddess in England.

Avebury henge, the largest stone circle in Britain, lies seventeen miles from Stonehenge, part of a sacred precinct that includes the earlier causeway enclosure of Windmill Hill, the West Kennet mound, and the Sanctuary, as well as the tumulus of Silbury Hill. At Avebury we see an evolving tradition that draws on the past rituals of its people yet moves at the same time to a religious vision that is increasingly articulated. There, the body of the Goddess, the earth, is both transformed and celebrated; the Avebury monuments evoke the interconnectedness of life and death in the Goddess. One of the earliest of the sacred sites is the Sanctuary on Overton Hill, overlooking the river Kennet, to the south of the later Silbury Hill; it was first built in 2900 B.C. and rebuilt over the next four hundred years. Originally a wood structure in the shape of two concentric circles and topped by a thatched roof, it was later rebuilt of stone in roughly the same shape. Many writers have speculated about the use of this building, perhaps an astronomical observatory, a communal dwelling place, or a structure for the enactment of female puberty rites. Burl has suggested that, given the Sanctuary's proximity to both water and the barrows, it may have been a charnel house, a place where the bodies of the dead were brought, the flesh washed and perhaps subjected to heat to accelerate decay so that the bones — cleansed by water and fire — could be buried or ceremonially handled.[30] When the Sanctuary was rebuilt in stone, a young person, perhaps a girl, was buried in a shallow grave in the inner ring. The body, its hands placed over its face, faced the east and the rising sun, possibly an offering to empower the rings. Red ocher — the consistent symbol of the blood of life in the Neolithic — was found buried at the Sanctuary.

Work on Silbury Hill, the tumulus raised on low ground a mile to the west of the Sanctuary, probably began around 2750 B.C. This monument was no mere piling up of earth and rubble but a painstaking construction, seven "drums," or layers, one on top of the other. It may well be that the layers were ritually symbolic: the first, clay with flints, is like the clay cores of the barrows and may suggest that the rituals of Silbury Hill were somehow

Silbury Hill

Built by human hands, the hill is a powerful expression of the energy of life hidden within the belly of the Goddess, eternally fecund; the hill may well be, as Michael Dames has suggested, the Pregnant Goddess herself.

involved with death. Turf and topsoil covered the clay core, along with a few sarsen boulders. On top of the boulders were found bone fragments, the ribs of either a red deer or ox, stag antlers, bits of bushes, and mistletoe. Burl suggests that these may have been representations "of the fecund world desired by these early farmers, a gathering together of fertile earth, vegetation, edible animals, flint and stone, a concentration of richness sealed under the great mound close to lifegiving water."[31] Chalk rubble comprised the succeeding layers until the final one, again composed of topsoil, rich with life.

Many of the women and men who labored on Silbury Hill probably died without seeing it completed, yet their vision was unified. Built by humanity, the Hill is nonetheless of the earth, a symbolic representation of the great power of the Goddess. The Hill is distinctly, deliberately different from not only the low land it sits on but from the other ritual monuments of Avebury, the low rectangular barrows. Its shape is evocative, whether we see the eye or breast of the Goddess, or, as Michael Dames has suggested, the squatting Goddess in labor.[32] Although the site was constructed by human hands, the life-giving aspect of the Goddess was symbolically expressed by the fact that the Hill gave birth to life — plants and grasses. It is possible that, in addition to its symbolic meanings, the flat top served as the altar where the first fruits of the harvest were offered to the Goddess.

Standing Stones of Callanish

On a promontory on the Isle of Lewis in the Hebrides stand the Standing Stones of Callanish; from the circle, the waters of the surrounding lochs can be seen in three directions, although the sea itself is hidden from view. The stones form a ring encircling a chambered tomb and a large stone; three single rows of stone and one double row or avenue approach the circle. It seems likely, as Aubrey Burl suggests, that the builders' intention was to create four full avenues, although the work was never completed.

While some scholars have suggested that the standing stones were aligned with the stars and the moon, the possibility that the rites performed here were connected to water remains. The stones, though, have kept their silence on this island. Is it possible, as Burl proposes, that they are "the result of solitude working upon the religious fervor of peoples whose lives were limited by their own island"?

Although the rites once practiced here have long since been forgotten, the sacrality of the stones was long preserved in local folklore: up through the last century, couples would make their marriage vows here.

The sacred landscape of Silbury Hill, though, acquired even more meaning with the building of the Avebury henge.

Two great avenues of standing stones, more than a mile and a half long, lead to a chalk bank on which stands an enormous circle of what was once a hundred stones surrounding two smaller stone circles. The bank is surrounded by a great ditch. The southern circle, made up of thirty stones, had, near its center, a high stone known as the Obelisk. At the base of the Obelisk were small pits filled with fertile soil, as well as human bones. A second double circle of stones — the outer ring made up of twenty-seven stones and the inner of twelve — was erected to the north; at the center stood a Cove made up of three huge slabs. The scale of the henge is enormous: the ditch encloses a 28½-acre site, and is 23 to 33 feet deep; the 190 sarsen slabs form a circle with a radius of 538 feet. Four entrances led into the Avebury Sanctuary, each marked by gigantic stones. At the southern entrance is Kennet Avenue, which begins at the Sanctuary. It is marked by double rows of stones, alternately pillar- and lozenge–shaped, perhaps symbolizing the male and female. Another processional road originated at a Cove on a hillock a mile away and passed over the Windbourne Stream before ending at the western entrance to the henge.

The size of the henge and the width of the processional avenues suggest that whatever ceremonies and rites were conducted at Avebury involved a great many people; it may have been a religious center that drew people from neighboring areas. The differ-

127

Ring of Brodgar, Stenness, Orkney, Scotland

One of England's largest stone circles — its diameter is equal to that of the inner circle at Avebury and that of New Grange — stands on a narrow isthmus a mile away from another henge, the Standing Stones of Stenness. Both are close to huge passage graves, encouraging the idea that complementary rituals, perhaps involving death and seasonal ceremonies of regeneration, took place here.

OPPOSITE PAGE:
Stone Formation on the Antrim Coast Road, Northern Ireland

ences between the northern and southern circles of stone suggest that different rites or, perhaps, different stages of a single rite were conducted in each. Certainly the pits filled with soil near the Obelisk suggest a rite of invocation to the Goddess' regenerative powers, while the Cove in the second circle reminds us that the Goddess is also the source of all death. Since the processional roads begin at the Sanctuary and another Cove, what was within the circle of stone at Avebury was symbolically linked to and echoed the procession's starting point. The two circles are enclosed within a still larger circle, reminding us of the eternal joining of death and regeneration.[33] The Goddess who reigns in the mound at Silbury is also the spirit of the charnel house, the Sanctuary.

Whether in considering the Avebury complex we imagine, as Michael Dames does, a complicated series of rites celebrating the Goddess in her cycles of life or, as Aubrey Burl does, a series of festivals and ceremonial processionals celebrating the cycle of death and regeneration in the harvest and the year itself, finally does not matter. The precise forms of rituals and worship here, as elsewhere, will always be a matter of conjecture and hypothetical reconstruction. But in the legacy of the sacred stones bequeathed to us, we can glimpse, in outline, if not detail, the Goddess in all of her glory, as source of all that is.

7 The Goddess at the Peak: Crete

Long before Arthur Evans' discovery in the first year of this century of the extraordinary civilization he named Minoan, a group of myths bore witness to the greatness of ancient Crete. Complicated and contradictory, and even cautionary, these myths hinted at mysterious, sacred truths, as well as at an exemplary way of life. On this island off the mainland of Greece, surrounded by the sparkling waters of the Aegean and Libyan seas, we find the ancient threads of the Goddess gathered for the last time into a single, radiant tapestry. The achievements of this civilization in sculpture, painting, architecture, and design exalt humanity's gift for creating beauty and harmony, and continue to inspire more than four thousand years later. On Crete the signs and symbols, rituals and rites of the Goddess, whose beginnings we have seen in Old Europe and its island outposts, find their fullest expression. And while Minoan civilization is also the last time in European history that the Goddess is in full ascendance, the Minoan vision, as the work of Vincent Scully has made clear, provides the underpinning for the Greek aesthetic and religion that would supersede it.[1]

All of the myths testify to Crete's sacredness of place and are reinforced by its unique geography. The terrain of the island is dominated by four principal groups of mountain ranges and notably by Mount Jouctas, the holy mountain of Minoan civilization. First a sanctuary of the Goddess and later the legendary birthplace of the infant Zeus, Mount Jouctas provided the focus for Minoan sacred architecture and itself symbolized the Goddess. The peaks of the highest Cretan mountains are snowcapped for part of the year and were, in ancient times, covered with verdant forests. Between the mountains lie narrow ravines bordered by cliffs. The seismic upheavals of the ages have created some three thousand caves and rock shelters that dot the landscape, many of them sacred. Fertile plains yield a wide variety of crops. Chestnut, oak, and cypress forests still grace the modern-day land, as do palm and cedar. Fragrant and medicinal herbs — dittany, marjoram, and thyme among them — grow wild on the rocky slopes. The Neolithic settlers would have found indigenous almond, quince, mulberry, lettuce, asparagus, and celery, as well as seas teeming with marine life, and land inhabited by deer, agrimi, pigeons, and partridge.[2] The contours of the land, the lush fertility of the earth, and the plenitudes of the sea must have signified the Goddess' nurturing presence on the island.

The Goddess of the Minoans was a deity of the earth, from whom all the gifts of nature flowed, as evidenced by the celebration of nature contained in Minoan art — detailing the exquisite grace of the dolphin, the delicate lily, the perfect symmetry of the shell — and in the forms of Minoan worship that began in caves and on the mountaintops

The Sacred Peak: Mount Jouctas Seen from the Air

and culminated in the spatial orientation of the palaces. It may seem ironic to recover the power of the Goddess in the beginnings of Zeus the sky god who superseded her, but the resonance of this myth is eloquent testimony to what the Goddess in her nurturing aspects must have meant to those who lived on Crete.

The Zeus left to us on Crete is not the powerful sky god of the Homeric epics but an infant spirited away from the threat of his Titan father, Cronos, by his mother, Rhea, daughter of the goddess of the earth, Gaia. Cronos swallowed his children to assure that he would not be overthrown. Rhea herself was closely identified with Gaia — indeed, sometimes indistinguishable from her — although she was also associated with vegetative power and harvest, as Demeter later would be. The myth stresses the earthbound origins of the ruler of the sky: born in one cave, identified variously as that of Mount Dikte or Mount Ida, and hidden from Cronos' murderous wrath in the Idaean, Zeus had the power of the ancient places sacred to the Goddess (the island itself, its caves, and later the peak Jouctas, which was held to be the burial place of Zeus) mythically conferred upon him.[3] Even though the myth begins the story of what is to be Zeus' ascendancy and dominance over the old Goddess, here on Crete it is the Goddess' power that shines through the details: in the figures of Rhea, the mother, and Gaia, the earth, who hides Zeus; in the life-protecting power of caves and peaks; and in the female attendant, the virgin Britomartis, or Dictynna (the Sweet Maiden aspect of the Goddess). The fierce male Curetes, guards who drown out the infant Zeus' cries by clashing swords and shields, do the Goddess' bidding; in later myths, they become her bodyguards, and still later become her priests, celebrating fertility in rituals. In this myth, it is the Goddess in her multifold aspects — as earth (Gaia), mother and source of life (Rhea), and virgin (Britomartis) — who gives Zeus life. Later ancillary myths about the infant Zeus' being nurtured by animals, either the goat or the bee (both of which are strongly associated with the Goddess) seem to make the same point.[4] While the myth validates Zeus, associating him with the Cretan Goddess, it also testifies to the Goddess' lasting power.[5]

It should scarcely surprise us that Cretan caves sacred to the Goddess in her aspect as protector of childbirth (Eileithyia) were used continuously as places of worship from the Neolithic to the fifth century B.C.

Crete was probably first colonized sometime around 6000 B.C. by settlers from Anatolia, who might have brought with them a form of Goddess worship similar in its outlines to that practiced at Çatal Hüyük. Certain aspects of later Minoan religion, such as the veneration of the bull and the bull's horns and the use of consistent symbols to designate

Bee Pendant from Mallia

The bee, like the butterfly, was a symbol of the regenerative power of the Goddess as early as the Neolithic. Ancient belief held that bees were born out of the dead carcass of the bull, making the bee a symbol of life emerging from death. This exquisite gold pendant was found in the funerary complex at Mallia.

Minoan Goddess with Poppies

Her raised arms announce that she is the Earth Mother, while her masked face reminds us she is numinous. Her diadem is crowned with poppies, indicating that she is also the Goddess of the Grain; the poppy, as Nilsson remarks, grows with corn in the fields, and it is pictured on rings and seals in the hands of the Goddess as a symbol of her fruits.

Horns of Consecration (Restored), Knossos

Apart from the double ax, no other sacral symbol occurs as frequently in Minoan civilization as the horns of consecration. Two pairs of stucco horns were found in the Shrine of the Double Axes; the fragments of colossal horns were found near the south entrance to Knossos. Rendered in clay, stone, stucco, and bronze, inscribed on stone and gems, painted on walls and vases, mounted on the facades of buildings, the horns denoted the sacred precinct, direct descendants of the actual bucrania of the shrines at Çatal Hüyük.

shrines, resonate with the symbols of Old Europe. These immigrants first lived in caves that also served as burial places, and then settled on the hill that later was to be the site of the great palace at Knossos. In addition to farming and hunting, they raised livestock that they had brought with them from Anatolia.[6] This settlement apparently flourished amid the abundant fertility of the island, and its culture, which seems to have become ceramic around 5600 B.C., continued without significant change for the next several thousand years. Then a second wave of settlers came, probably from Anatolia and Libya in 3500 B.C., bringing with them the sensibility that would culminate in Minoan civilization. Crete's geographical position on sea routes linking three continents meant that ideas and commodities from Asia, Africa, and Europe reached it.[7]

The Goddess as she is finally realized on Crete is as varied as the land she dominated, and it is that multiplicity which reminds us that, while we may trace the achievements of a people back through their inherited roots and through their contacts with others, the full flowering of a civilization is always possessed of a unique stamp. We do not know whether the Goddess went by a single name or many, but as R. W. Willetts points out, the question is unimportant since her pervasive influence is evident from the complexity of symbolism and associations.[8] Her domain extended over all the eye could see: mountain, sky, earth, sea. Among the emblems of her presence were the baetylic pillar and sacred trees; stalactites and stalagmites; animals, birds, and snakes; poppies and lilies; seashells carved from stone and in relief. Painted seashells covered the floors of the shrine treasury at Knossos, and tritons were probably blown to invoke the Goddess. Her epiphany as the Goddess of regeneration is symbolized by the dove and by the butterfly that rises from the body of the sacrificial bull. The similarity in shape of the butterfly and the double ax complicates the meaning of both. Marija Gimbutas holds that the butterfly is "the embodiment of the principle of Transformation" and that the double ax was "originally an hourglass-shaped Goddess of Death and Regeneration."[9] Of all the Minoan symbols of the Goddess, the sacred double ax is the most pervasive.

Rendered in bronze and gold, lead and stone, with ornamentation and without, depicted on vessels, gems, and pithoi and crowning sacral buildings, the double ax is ubiquitous. On the Hagia Triada Sarcophagus, its long handle, carried by a priestess, is covered in vegetation. Sometimes a leaf grows from its shaft, or plants grow up its sides. Sometimes the axes themselves, rendered without their handles, form the pattern on a vessel. On pillars and stone blocks of sacred buildings, the ax is reduced to a double triangle, inscribed or scratched on stone. The double ax was called the *labrys*, and when the Greeks found the ruins of what had been the palace of Knossos — a veritable maze — they called it the House of the Double Axes, or the labyrinth.

While the double ax as a tool probably had a practical use in Minoan civilization, the *labrys* is a ritual instrument from early Minoan times onward. Usually it is rendered in material that is too soft or fragile to be of practical application; while some of the axes are huge, others fit in the palm of the hand, with only a pin for a handle. It seems possible that the ax was once the instrument of sacrifice in Minoan religion and accrued greater symbolic meaning as a result. Through the successive stages of Minoan civilization, the double ax lost none of its sacrality. At the cave of Psychro, double axes were thrust into the crevices between the stalagmite pillars of the lower cave. At Knossos, Evans thought (on the basis of a fresco) that double axes had been stuck into wooden pillars within a shrine, suggesting that an act of invocation was involved, calling the Goddess from her caves and peak sanctuaries into the created labyrinth.

The double ax is *never* depicted in the hands of a male god,[10] a fact that clearly separates Minoan symbolism from the Indo-European tradition, in which it is a masculine weapon. Jacquetta Hawkes sees the ax primarily as a sexual symbol, reminding us of the ancient use of the triangle and double triangle as female signs; she suggests too that the frequent depiction of the double ax between the horns of the bull as well as the horns of consecration is primarily sexual in meaning.[11]

Who is the Goddess honored on Crete? A huntress, a goddess of sports, who presides over ritual dancing; a household goddess ringed by snakes, a palace goddess, a

**Peak Sanctuary at
Mount Petsofa, Zakros**

by Marija Gimbutas. Each animal symbolizes the Goddess in her regenerative aspects, and each amulet may well have had a slightly different function or meaning. The pig, a sacrificial animal on Crete and elsewhere, may have represented the Goddess as the intercessor between the living and the dead; the bird, the Goddess in her chthonic aspect; the cow and hedgehog (representing the power of the uterus), symbols of the Goddess' regenerative energy.[18]

Sometime between the end of the Early Minoan period (2400 B.C.) and the beginning of the Middle Minoan (2200 B.C.), the worship of the Goddess became communal, and we find the establishment of peak sanctuaries, the most important of which lies atop the sacred Mount Jouctas. Once again, the location of these sacred places, the simplicity of their architecture, and the rites practiced (figurines tucked into the crevices of the rock, penetrating, as it were, the body of the Goddess) remind us that the Minoan Goddess remains centered in the earth. It was a religion, as Gertrude Levy so eloquently put it, that was "unusually detached from formal bonds, but emotionally binding in its constant effort to establish communion with the elemental powers."[19] Many of these sanctuaries stood within a circular or oval area surrounded by an enclosure wall. The basic design is that of an antechamber and a shrine room, although a few sanctuaries are more complex. There is some evidence for the establishment at this time of presiding priestesses or priests.

The rites of the peak sanctuaries suggest both a continuity with Early Minoan practices and a further complication of ritual. Ash deposits imply that the rites involved fire, although Keith Branigan suggests that these fires probably did not burn throughout the year but were lit on specific occasions when the sanctuaries were visited.[20] The bones of small animals found here may indicate early sacrificial practices that were followed by a sacramental meal. Figurines of a wide variety of domestic and wild animals were discovered in the sanctuaries in great numbers, some placed within crevices, some found in the ash deposits of the fires. Again, the symbolism of Old Europe suggests that some of these animal figures may be epiphanies of the Goddess herself, or may have been used to invoke certain of her life-giving aspects. It is possible, too, that the wild animals symbolize her fruits, although we cannot know whether they were meant as tokens of thanks or as invocation for her continued beneficence. Some, like the terra-cotta representations of the rhinoceros beetle, may have been considered sacred to the Goddess. (While certain scholars have assumed the figurines of beetles were present so that the suppliant might receive relief from a noxious pest, Platon suggests that, since they were also depicted in clay models of shrines and shown climbing on worshippers, the beetles were themselves sacred.)[21] Figurines of complete human bodies, and of individual limbs and even bisected bodies, invite the conclusion that some of the rites involved invocations of the Goddess' protection or for help in healing, or oracular rites through dream incubation. Such figures of pierced bodies and limbs were discovered at the Hal Saflieni Hypogeum in Malta and at later Greek oracular shrines.[22]

A rhyton found at the palace of Zakros depicts a sanctuary and gives us an image of what these holy sites might have looked like. The central altar of the peak sanctuaries might have stood at the center of a courtyard, the enclosing walls of which were crowned with horns of consecration. On the rhyton, sacred symbols may indicate the Goddess' presence: she may be represented by the birds that alight on the horns, or by the baetyl, flanked by two pairs of wild goats. At Zakros, the Goddess at the peak, in her aspect of Mistress of the Wild Animals, has wild goats, rather than lions, as her attendants.

We will probably never know whether communion with the Goddess at the peak sanctuaries was achieved by billows of smoke arcing into the sky, by symbolic rebirth in fire, or by dream incubation. What we can grasp now, however, is the potent vision of the

Goddess at the peak, the Goddess of the mountain, an extension of her epiphany as the sacred pillar connecting the earth and the sky. Pictured on Minoan seals and gems, the ritual libations to the deity are poured over peak and pillar alike. On a seal from Knossos, the Goddess is seen between guardian lions on a peak crowned by horns of consecration: the goddess of childbirth as well as, in Gimbutas' words, "the incarnation of the fertility of Nature."[23]

The Goddess worshipped in the peak sanctuaries assumed more than one aspect: Earth Mother, sacred virgin, or even the Snake or Household Goddess. In the next stage of Minoan civilization, she will find her greatest and most majestic articulation.

The building of the first palaces in approximately 2000 B.C. begins the final and glorious moment of Minoan history. Arthur Evans' discovery of the remains of this astonishing society explained for the first time why, long after it had become a provincial backwater of mainland Greece, Crete continued to tug at the strings of humanity's imagination. Hesiod, writing in the eighth century, described a land of plenty, where humanity lived in harmony without war. Plato's descriptions of the island of Atlantis in his *Critias* tantalize us with their similarities to Minoan civilization as we now know it. For some six hundred years, the civilization of Crete possessed a vision of life that did not require pastoral inventions of the poetic imagination: art and artifact both proclaim a vital, exuberant vision of life, fully in harmony with nature. At the center of this vision is the Minoan Goddess, whose presence illuminates at every turn. Minoan civilization, as well as its art, reverberates with the grace, calm, and joy of this culture, so different from our own. That it honored women was of course revelatory, but this is only part of what continues to amaze and inspire us. It is the central presence of the deity, the Goddess, that, as Kostas Papaioannou has written, renders the artistic vision of Minoan life remarkable, for "it reflects no awareness of the terrifying gap that can separate the human from the transcendental. It is as if the quest for eternity has been resolved by affirming the divine favor of existence itself. A hymn to the glory of nature, perceived as a goddess, seems to flush from every quarter; the agony of death and the rictus of disease are nowhere to be seen."[24]

That steady rootedness in the forces of nature commands our attention, as does all that the rootedness implies: an acceptance of the cycle of life, and of life and death perceived not in opposition but in eternal linkage. Surely too that equilibrium is reflected in the balancing double symbols we see in Minoan art: the two double axes held in the Goddess' hands, the bull's double horns of consecration, the two snakes curling on the Goddess' arms, the double patterns of snake, egg, and nautilus on seals and stones.[25]

Amphorae, Knossos

The building complex contained twenty long corridors, or "magazines," filled with vessels that held oil and grain and other reserves.

The Palace of Knossos

To modern eyes, there is perhaps a patent contradiction in Minoan civilization, where the energy of a changing, sophisticated society is nonetheless coupled with an adherence to older forms, ancient ways of seeing. Gertrude Levy draws attention to this by reminding us that the Minoans never built temples but continued to perform their rites "through the splendid epochs of their material achievement on mountain peaks, in caves,

The West Bastion, Knossos

in household chapels, and rustic shrines."[26] The rituals themselves continued to draw on the forms of the past, maintaining the age-old association of the Goddess with the sacred tree, the pillar, and the cavern, and representing her symbolically by the double ax, the horns of consecration, and the snake. The palaces of Knossos, Mallia, Phaistos, Gournia, and Zakros were built (and rebuilt, for all save the later palace of Zakros were destroyed around 1700 B.C., probably by an earthquake) to epitomize both sides of the Minoan coin, the flourishing of human achievements subjugated visually and symbolically to the elemental powers.

The splendors of the palace at Knossos are testimony to a civilization with a marvelous aesthetic sensibility empowered by wealth. Production and commerce in Minoan Crete were sufficiently complicated to require record-keeping, no longer written in pictographs but in the as yet undeciphered Linear A. Fine work and technological skill abounded, as seen in Minoan lapidaries' detailed miniatures executed on seals and stones without the aid of a magnifying glass. As a complex of buildings designed for ceremony, rite, and habitation, Knossos is still astounding today. Apart from its ceremonial areas, it contained administrative offices; rooms for the storage of grain and oil; workshops for stone carvers, potters, and metalworkers; and also remarkable living quarters, full of light, with majestic staircases and terraces. Comfort was part of the Minoan vision, reflected in the elaborate under-the-floor and gutter drainage facilities, and even flushing lavatories. Frescoed walls and painted surfaces delight the eye in what seems to be a continual celebration of both the human and the natural world. The ceremonial aspects of Knossos are also highly complex, seeming to reach back in time to the traditions of the Neolithic while nonetheless giving the rites a sophisticated stamp. What appeared a haphazard pattern of development and design to earlier commentators has been shown by Vincent Scully to be a conscious use of the symbols of the Goddess in both the natural landscape and man-made forms.

The landscape elements Scully delineates are present at all the palace sites: an enclosed valley in which the palace is set; a conical or mounded hill on a north-south axis to the palace; a high, double-peaked or cleft mountain on the same axis, some distance beyond the hill. As Scully discovered, the features of the mountain "create a profile which is basically that of a pair of horns, but it may sometimes also suggest raised arms or wings, the female cleft, or even, at some sites, a pair of breasts." These words bring to mind the lineage of the Minoan Goddess with startling clarity, and with a vividness that spans the millennia: she is the Minoan Poppy Goddess, sprung from the Goddess of the Neolithic and of Lespugue, the Goddess of Çatal Hüyük and of Sardinia and Malta, recognizable in all of her shapes. These natural forms, in Scully's words, are "the basic architecture of the palace complex. They define its space and focus it." The constructed elements of the palace — the labyrinthine passage, the columned pavilion, and the pillared cave — all echo the traditional symbols of the Goddess.[27]

"All these forms," Scully writes, "both the natural and the constructed, can be shown to relate to what we otherwise know of Minoan religion and its dominant goddess, so that the natural and the man-made create one ritual whole, in which man's part is defined and directed by the sculptural masses of the land and is subordinate to its rhythms."

Older traditions and sacred places are skillfully integrated into the rites of the Minoan palaces. Within the created sacred space of the palace at Knossos, the Goddess' peak sanctuary on Mount Jouctas would be visible both to the mind's eye and, in the course of a ritual procession, literally. At the palace of Phaistos, the sacred site is Mount Ida, site of

The Great South Propylon at Knossos

The frescoes depict the sacred procession, the images echoing the movement of those who walked in the sacred precinct on the way to the Grand Staircase.

the Kamares Cave and the Idaean Cave; at Mallia, it is Mount Dikte, and the cave sacred to the Goddess where the infant Zeus was later said to have been born; at Zakros, it is the peak sanctuary of Piskokephalo. The religious life of the palaces did not supersede that of the peak sanctuaries but conjoined with these older sacred places. Nicholas Platon has suggested that, at Zakros at least, pilgrimages to the peak sanctuary probably took place on fixed days, as did visits to the sacred caves.[28]

Although there are variations among them, the Minoan palaces — including Knossos, which is three times as large as any other — were organized around a large, elongated central court with main wings on the west (containing shrine rooms and cult areas as well as storerooms) and on the east (containing the living quarters of the royal family as well as ceremonial rooms). The design of the palaces is deliberately labyrinthine, partly to accommodate processions, an important element of Minoan ritual. In the absence of written records, our knowledge of Minoan rites is derived and reconstructed from artifacts found in situ. From lustral basins, a rite of purification for those entering the sacred precinct has been assumed; the spring well at Zakros, which contained an offering of olives to the deity, might also have been a shrine. The pouring of libations from rhytons as part of the ritual is portrayed by images on seals and evidenced by the discovery at the various palaces of the elaborate rhytons, some in the shape of bulls' heads. Both bloodless and blood sacrifices were part of the rites of the Minoans, as was the bull dance performed in the huge central court (190 by 92 feet) of the palace of Knossos.

Vincent Scully's masterful re-creation of the sacred procession at Knossos reminds us of the Goddess' roots and the role theater has always played in the rituals of humanity. The ceremonial entrance to the palace lies on the north side, with its "theatral" road and narrow paths and steps that must be approached in a single file. From the steps, two possible processional routes emerge, each with its own visual and symbolic implications. The first takes the participants into a pillared hall, up a ramp, and finally into the long open court, where, in Scully's words, the eye is directed "toward the sacred mountain of the goddess and emphasizes the natural order derived from her." The second path, while following a more labyrinthine route, puts the suppliants directly on axis with the mountain, moving from light into dark, then from confined space into openness. The narrow path along the west side of the palace has both the nearer hill and Jouctas in view; the open space of the West Court would divide, giving way to an altar that, in turn, would give way to the west porch with a single column — symbol of the Goddess' presence — enclosed within its walls. From this open space to a narrow enclosure lined with processional frescoes, the line of humanity would enter a dark space, then weave through the propylaea (with the horned mountain and the emblematic Horns of Consecration crowning the facade

Bull's Head Rhyton

Sacred libations were poured from this magnificent vessel, made of black soapstone, with eyes of jasper and rock crystal; the horns, here restored, were probably made of gilded wood.

The Grand Staircase at Knossos

The staircase was once lit by a light well supported by columns. At the bottom of the staircase is the Hall of Colonnades.

of the palace again in view), and into the shadows of the main columned hall. A narrow stairway led to the light of the center court, where the bull dance took place.[29]

One of the great symbols of Minoan religion, the bull reaches back in time to the cave walls of the Paleolithic and to Çatal Hüyük for many of its meanings. From Old Europe comes the association with regeneration and symbols aligned with energy: snake coils, concentric circles, eggs, cupmarks, antithetic spirals, and life columns. Unlike Indo-European symbolism, which portrays the bull as specifically masculine strength and energy, the symbolism of Old Europe connects the horns with the regenerative power of the female (perhaps, as some have suggested, because of the similarities in shape between the female organs of reproduction and the head and horns of the bull).[30] That Minoan

The Queen's Megaron, Knossos

civilization is a direct legatee of the traditions of Çatal Hüyük is made clear not only from the palace architecture, which melds the secular with the sacral as did its predecessor's, but also from the bull crania that demarcate the sacred shrine. At Çatal Hüyük, the Goddess gives birth to the bull; in Crete, the double ax springs from its horns. It is in this context that the libations drunk from rhytons in the shape of the bull — perhaps even containing the blood of the sacrificed animal — must be understood. The complexity of the bull as symbol, central to the Goddess, is nowhere as clear as in the Minoan rite of the bull dance.

The bull dance or game was a celebration of the Goddess' raw energy as it is embodied in nature, not a test of cunning or endurance as is the modern-day bullfight, which symbolizes the victory of man over brute force. Although it may well have ended in the solemn sacrifice of the animal, the dance, in Scully's words, "celebrated both men and women together as accepting nature's law, adoring it, adding to their own power insofar as they seized it close and adjusted their rhythms to its force."[31] The fresco from Knossos depicting the bull dance has a quiet, stylized grace that reminds us of the stateliness of ritual. The dancers faced danger in the dance as they grasped the horns of the bull, just as humanity must face the danger implicit in the Goddess' power over both life and death.

The procession through the palace might have come to an end in the dark, cavelike Shrine of the Double Axes, and so, in Scully's description, "the processional movement from light to dark to light and dark again — culminating as it does in the innermost cavern shrine where were found at once the hollow earth of the goddess and the pillar which both enters and supports the earth and is thus also here — makes the Minoan palace as a whole that ceremonial labyrinth around the secret place which the Greeks remembered in their myths."[32]

It is the true harmony with nature in all its aspects that illuminates the Minoan vision, the connection between the created interior space, the solemnity of ritual, and the exterior landscape of the Goddess; the created forms within echoing those without. It is a vision, surely, that challenges our twentieth-century distinctions between the sacred and the mundane. Nanno Marinatos' study of Minoan sacrifices reminds us again that a sacred enclosure could be indicated by a number of sacred objects, such as horns of consecration, a baetyl, a grove of trees, and that indeed sacrifice could and probably did take place

Bull-Leaping Fresco from Knossos

148

Snake Goddesses

(c. 1600 B.C.)

The elaborate ceremonial clothes of these two statuettes evoke the solemnity of Minoan ritual; the complication of pattern and flounce endows them with a quiet sense of grandeur. They are possessed, too, of what Jacquetta Hawkes called a "frank sexuality." Their breasts are pushed high by their bodices and in their prominence are clearly meant to be seen and admired. The statuettes are symbols of strength and fecundity.

The coiling snake is the ancient symbol of sacred energy, primordial and mysterious. Living in crevices in the earth, it is of the earth, both source of all life and the burial place of the dead. It is also a symbol of life and death, because in its seasonal sloughing off of its skin and hibernation, it both dies and comes to life again. The Snake Goddess at the far left brandishes the power of the snake in her fists, and the sternness of her expression reminds us that if she is the source of all life, she is equally the repository of all death. This is the death-wielding Goddess, whose power is expressed in the earthquakes that shake and tumble down the walls of the palaces that humanity has built; formal and unyielding, she has a leopard or lioness on her headdress.

The Goddess at the near left is enveloped by a serpentine embrace; she holds in her hand the head of a snake that goes up one arm, across her shoulders, and down the other arm. Around her girdled waist, two snakes encircle her. She is the sacred energy incarnate. Her face betrays none of the other Goddess' stern power but is, instead, almost serene, reflecting her ability to harness the snake's sacred power.

In these figures from Knossos, the Snake Goddess is so personified that some scholars have questioned whether the statuettes actually might represent priestesses instead. The degree of human personification is, more likely, a meaningful confusion that represents intimacy with the Goddess in this epiphany. In European folklore and tradition, the snake was also seen as the guardian and protector of the house, and in this context, some scholars, Nilsson among them, hold that the Snake Goddess was venerated in the interiors of houses and in the palatial shrines as the special domestic goddess. She may also have been worshipped at the earlier peak sanctuaries as well; vessels found there show stylized loops that represent the coils of the snake, and one anthropomorphic jug has a snake draped over its shoulders.

inside and outside, with movable sacrificial tables at various sites appropriate to the invocation of the Goddess.[33] Was the mimetic character of the natural sacral forms — the stalagtites echoed in the column, the cave recalled in the shrine — meant to call the Goddess forth in one of her epiphanies, from her place on the peak into the created space? Can we imagine priestesses blowing on tritons to call her forth?

Scully's analysis of the Minoan palaces answers an old question. What had surprised Arthur Evans and others who were working backward in time from the Greek temples, which were created to house images of the deities, was the absence on Crete of elaborate, specifically religious structures. Scale and grandeur are notably absent in Minoan civilization. The Shrine of the Double Axes, for example, measures only one and a half square meters (roughly twenty-five square feet), and it is divided into three parts at different levels. Vessels stood in the main part of the room, and beyond, on a raised dais, was a square offering table with tripod legs. At the end of the room a ledge ran from wall to wall, and on it were placed two pairs of white stucco horns of consecration, several Goddess figures (one bell-shaped, one holding a dove), and images of female and male votaries. The shrine at Gournia, apparently a public one, was only four meters by three (roughly thirteen feet by nine). It too had a raised dais with a three-legged table at its center. Images of bird and snake heads were found there, as well as a fragment of a pithos decorated with a double ax.[34] What roles these small shrines played can only be guessed at from other evidence pertaining to ritual.

The elaborate sacral dress of priestesses indicated on frescoes and seals seems to suggest that rites of invocation, such as the blowing of the triton, sacred dancing, and ceremonies including boughs, were part of Minoan worship, and that the Goddess could be invoked not only by trees and pillars but by the acts of her human female attendants. In the later stages of Minoan civilization, the close connection between the Goddess and her priestesses is emphasized by dress: the Mother of the Mountains depicted in the seal from Knossos is, like her human counterparts of the frescoes, bare-breasted and wearing a flounced skirt. The Snake Goddess found in the Central Palace Sanctuary (and the one now in the Boston Museum of Fine Arts, whose provenance is unknown) wears sumptuously detailed garments like those worn by the women of the frescoes. In addition, faience models of robes and girdles found in the Sanctuary appear to have been votive offerings to the Goddess, pieces of a sacred wardrobe. All this suggests that the later rituals may well have included the priestesses themselves personifying the Goddess, becoming through dress and perhaps ritual dance representations of the deity herself in human form.[35]

Did the Minoans have a vision of a life after death? Was a general idea of regeneration within the womb of the Goddess finally superseded by a more precisely realized one, that of a terrestrial, or extraterrestrial, paradise? Was the idea of Elysium possibly of Minoan origin? For the past century, scholars have looked toward the Hagia Triada Sarcophagus for answers to this question, a lively debate that continues to this day. The sarcophagus dates from the very end of the Minoan period, painted in the same

Palace of Gournia

Just as Knossos had its sacred mountain, so too the ruins of the central court at Gournia show Mount Ida rising majestically to the north. Gournia is set within hills, giving it, in Vincent Scully's words, "a sense of absolute enclosure by the earth."

The Palace of Phaistos

The ruins of this Minoan
palace occupy a pine-shaded
hill overlooking the Mesara
Plain, a site inhabited since
the Neolithic. From the
palace, the sacred peak of
Mount Ida is clearly visible.

152

century in which all of the Minoan palaces were destroyed in a cataclysmic event, sometime between 1450 and 1400 B.C. The style of the painting on the sarcophagus was decidedly influenced by contemporaneous Egyptian art, and scholars have shown that the Egyptians and the Cretans were in contact with each other and maintained a mutual respect.[36]

The long sides of the limestone coffin depict two different, but related, scenes. On one panel, we see what appears to be a funeral procession, men bearing grave goods (images of bulls and a ship model) in their arms and walking toward a still figure who stands before a tree and what is probably a tomb. On the same panel, but facing in the opposite direction, a priestess pours the contents of a vessel into a larger vessel set between two pillars with double axes. A dove perches on each double ax. The priestess is attended by two men, one of them a musician. On the far panel, a procession of women is led by a flute player toward a bull bound on a sacrificial table and bleeding into a vessel. Underneath the table are two apparently frightened goats. Beyond the dying bull, a woman offers libations at an altar, before a double ax on which a bird perches. Beyond the altar, in turn, is an enclosure surrounding a sacred tree, the enclosure itself crowned by the horns of consecration. Bird, tree, double ax: the familiar symbols of the Minoan Goddess on these panels denote her role in the proceedings. On the narrow ends of the coffin, however, she herself appears: on one side driving a horse-drawn chariot, accompanied by an attendant, and on the other driving a griffin-drawn chariot. On the wings of one of the griffins, a dark bird with outspread wings perches; the Goddess here is accompanied by another figure, this one with a gray pallor suggesting death.

Are these panels, as Levy and Hawkes have suggested, images of human death and rebirth, the first attended by the horse-drawn Goddess and the second accomplished by the griffin-driven Goddess with the dead man's soul in the form of a bird perched on the griffin's wing?[37] Or are they, as Jane Harrison thought, symbolic ritual renderings of the passing of the old year and the beginning of the new, of winter and spring, death and rebirth, illustrating a rite of vegetation?[38] The precise meaning of these painted scenes will never be known to us, but the Hagia Triada Sarcophagus confirms the Goddess' continued presence in Late Minoan art in the old symbolic forms and in a personified epiphany. It also reflects the complexity of the rituals accompanying her worship: again the old forms of the double ax, the horns of consecration, the sacred tree, but this time incorporating music and sacrifice.

Minoan civilization ended abruptly, the victim of an apparent catastrophe that has been the subject of considerable debate. Among the possible disasters suggested are invasion

Agia Triada Sarcophagus
(Detail)

This limestone coffin, its surface plastered and then painted, was found at the villa of Agia Triada near Phaistos. The villa commanded views of the Mesara Plain, Mount Ida, and the sea.

from the mainland of Greece, plague, and an earthquake of almost unimaginable proportions emanating from the volcanic eruption of Thera on the island of Santorini. The catastrophe, whatever its source, left all the palaces destroyed, all save Knossos never to be inhabited again.

Nicholas Platon's excavations of the palace of Zakros — a palace stopped in the stream of time, the objects of both ritual and daily life abruptly abandoned as the inhab-

The Palace of Zakros

Set in a valley at the eastern
extremity of Crete near a
calm, natural port, the Zakros
palace had, like the other
Minoan palaces, a central
court with main wings
west and east, as well as
secondary northern and
southern wings. The West
Wing contained the shrine
and cult rooms, while
the living quarters and the
ceremonial hall were in the
East Wing. Zakros is smaller
than the other palaces; its
Central Court occupies an
area roughly one-third the
size of the court at Knossos.
The site yielded many
examples of double axes set
onto bases; the double ax
also surmounted the religious
structures, while incised
double axes were found on
the walls of the entrance
to the West Wing from the
Central Court.

itants fled for their lives — have provided evidence for his moving re-creation of a final, desperate negotiation between the people and their Goddess. The first eruption of Thera probably occurred about 1500 B.C., and although damage to most of the Minoan centers was probably extensive, it was not irreparable. For the next fifty years, life went on. But after the subsequent disaster, the final destruction was, in Platon's words, "sudden and complete." Storerooms left full of provisions, ceremonial rooms with recently used ritual equipment, kettles and pots on kitchen hearths, raw materials and works-in-progress by artisans — all attest to sudden catastrophe.

Platon's excavations found special offerings to the deity, pieces of pumice in conical cups among others, and he suggests that the arrival of pumice on these shores — a harbinger of the disaster, which would have been remembered from the eruption fifty years earlier — prompted the inhabitants to try to appease the chthonic powers. In his words, "Ceremonies were conducted in the shrines, and offerings were made at the points where the presence of these divinities was most felt — at the sources of water, in the depths of sacred caves, in the underground repositories, in the lustral basins where the steps led down to the underworld."[39] The vision of the consequences of a volcanic eruption equal in force to that of Krakatoa in the nineteenth century is terrible indeed: thick ash would have covered and destroyed the vegetation; sources of water would have dried up or been polluted; endemic and epidemic diseases would have decimated the remaining population. For those who remained, the only choice would have been to abandon the island completely, and evidence of Minoan migration elsewhere suggests precisely this outcome.

With the end of Minoan civilization, the tapestry of ancient threads, the worship of the Goddess, is torn and sundered. The old ways of the Goddess did not, of course, disappear, but were absorbed into the ethos of a new, warfaring people from the mainland, the Mycenaeans, who took the ruins of Knossos as their own. Aspects of the old forms of worship were transformed to serve new needs, and the symbols of the old order became the signs of the new. The light that had been Minoan civilization, however, continued to shine in humanity's imagination, transformed by new myths but still unextinguished.

8 *Homer and the Goddess*

By the year 2000 B.C. the Indo-Europeans had settled on the Greek mainland, warrior tribes led by warrior kings who prized the cult of the hero and military victory. They were traders, too, coming into contact with the rest of the island civilizations of the Aegean. Their culture, which we now call Mycenaean, was well established by the sixteenth century, and sometime around 1500 B.C. they either vanquished the Minoans on Crete by force or took over the island already decimated by natural disaster, ruling for the next fifty years until the virtual destruction of the palaces. They brought with them their own pantheon of gods. Chief among them was the sky god Zeus, but Hera, Demeter, Athena, Poseidon, and Dionysus were also included, as the tablets written in Linear B tell us.[1] We know, too, that despite the striking and obvious differences between the peaceful Minoan ethos and that of the warrior kings, they had imitated Minoan forms and absorbed them even before their occupation of Crete.

It is a story full of paradox and contradiction. And while this period of human history traces the final desiccation of the rich culture of the Goddess that began in the Paleolithic era, culminated in Old Europe, and survived in the island cultures, we find traces of the Goddess throughout. In human history, old beliefs are rarely eradicated by new ones, even when imposed by force. As Marija Gimbutas reminds us, the process is instead "a gradual hybridization of two different symbolic systems."[2] While the Mycenaeans made their worldly power clear, reveled in their material goods and achievements, and buried their kings within high walls with masks of gold preserving their individual features, they nonetheless wanted to live and die under the Goddess' protection. As Vincent Scully notes, they "seemed to want to have life both ways, to act and be protected all the same," glorifying the martial achievements of the individual and yet subscribing to the natural order presided over by the Goddess. Scully is undoubtedly right in locating the beginnings of the great spiritual and intellectual conflict of the Greeks, establishing the boundaries between the realm of man and that of the gods, in Mycenaean times.[3]

In Minoan Crete, the palaces were unfortified and the peaks and high hills were the domain of the Goddess. Whether this was a consequence of the Minoans' essentially peaceful nature or of the existence of the greatest navy in the Aegean or both has been a topic of some debate. The Mycenaeans, however, needed fortifications on high to protect their goods and guard against their enemies, and they needed the view from higher up of who and what were approaching below. What had been exclusively the Goddess' sacred precinct therefore at Mycenae became the site for a citadel of man, built on an acropolis controlling the pass that led into the Argive Plain, a fortress with walls so huge and

The Lion's Gate

The relief of the two lions, carved from a single block of gray limestone, has a mass and weight that dominate our vision. The now missing heads of the lions might well have been made out of another material, as dowels in the necks suggest, perhaps of bronze or wood or even a finer stone. Sinclair Hood suggests that since the top of the relief above the columns is flat and has a dowel hole in it, the column might well have been crowned by a pair of birds or even horns of consecration.

imposing that the later Greeks assumed that the ruins of Mycenae had been built by the one-eyed giant, the Cyclops.

The Lion's Gate illustrates the Mycenaean paradox. Its huge walls, once forty feet high and twenty feet thick, protect and give way to the Upper Grave Circle, and it is first and foremost a testament to man in life and in death. Yet the gate itself, once probably hung with huge bronze doors that rendered the structure impervious to attacks by battering rams, is crowned by an epiphany familiar to us from Minoan Crete: two lions, their forepaws resting on an altar, stand on either side of a pillar, the aniconic form of the Goddess. Her protection presumably extended to the palace of the warlord that lay farther up the hill.

But the culture of kings that was Mycenae itself would fall, as the earlier invaders were themselves overrun by other Indo-European tribes, who brought with them their own gods; by 1100 B.C. the Minoan-Mycenaean world was eclipsed. Three hundred years later, a new culture emerged that would yield the civilization we call Greek, also the result of a mix of old and new ideas. The process of hybridization, of transformation, of the power and precincts of the Goddess is complex, absorbing the old and yet distancing it at the same time. So the attributes of the Goddess become those of the Greek goddesses of the pantheon, while myth and legend begin to retell the stories of the Goddess in ways that justify the new order and disenfranchise the old. The cluster of later myths that revolve around Crete provide telling examples of how older symbols are first robbed of ancient meanings and then reinvested with new ones.

If the bull in Minoan life is the symbol of the Goddess' regenerative power, then in the later myth of Europa and Zeus it is no accident that Zeus the sky god takes on its shape, seducing the naive Europa with its beauty and then carrying her forcibly across the sea to Crete. There is implicit violence in this myth: the beneficent regenerative power of the Goddess has been distorted into brute force, a mythic act that engenders three off-spring: Minos, Rhadamanthys, and Sarpedon.

According to legend, Minos was the ruler of Crete, said to have governed the island and the rest of the Aegean three generations before the Trojan War. He supposedly ruled for nine years at Knossos before retiring to a sacred cave where he received instruction from Zeus, his father. His legendary wisdom is reflected in his role as judge of the dead in the underworld in Homer's *Odyssey* (XI, 569); and both Herodotus and Thucydides, turning myth into patriarchal history, credit him with the equity of the Cretan constitution, as well as Crete's naval supremacy. Yet the Minos of myth was also arrogant and disrespectful of the gods. Poseidon sent him a white bull to sacrifice; instead, Minos offered up a lesser animal. In revenge, Poseidon contrived to have Minos' wife, Pasiphae (her

Head of Athena (Detail)

Martial Athena: protector and ally of the hero.

160

name, meaning "the all-shining," suggests that she was a moon goddess),[4] fall in love with the bull. With the help of Daedalus, master artisan, she had a contrivance in the shape of a cow fashioned, which permitted her to mate with the bull. From that union came the Minotaur, half man, half beast. According to myth, the master craftsman Daedalus then built a labyrinth — that is, the Goddess' House of the Double Axes — to house the Minotaur and its mother. Thus, the greatness of the Goddess' precinct at Knossos is degraded to a dark secret place fit only to hide a monster.

But it is the hero's tale of Theseus, who slays the Minotaur, that most vividly and finally recounts the symbolic vanquishing of the Goddess' sacred precinct and, ultimately, her power. Before coming to Crete to meet the challenge of the Minotaur, this son of the king of Athens had already established himself as a hero, conquering monsters, human and bestial, in the pattern of Greek myth that is echoed in other heroic cycles. In our context, however, it is the figure of Ariadne who arrests our attention. Daughter of Minos and Pasiphae, Ariadne (whose name means "all holy") falls in love with Theseus and gives him the thread that permits him to penetrate the labyrinth, kill the Minotaur, and depart in safety.

Gold Funerary Mask, Mycenae

The image of the male warrior, preserved for eternity in gold, reminds us of the differences between the warlord's citadel and the sacred mountain of the Goddess. Yet these warlords sought her protection nonetheless.

As her name suggests, Ariadne is no mere mortal. In the *Iliad*, Homer's description of the shield of Achilles includes the "dancing floor" fashioned for Ariadne by Daedalus in the "wide spaces" of Knossos, as well as a description of a dance performed by young women and women wearing sacral clothes and anointed with oil, bringing "gifts of oxen." He mentions too acrobats who lead "the measures of song and dance."[5] Surely the sacrificial animals, the ritual dance, and perhaps even the acrobats (are they bull leapers?) identify Ariadne with the Goddess of Knossos whom, as Nilsson reminds us, the dance honored.[6] Ariadne as the Minoan Goddess empowers Theseus ("he who endures"), as shown by the weapon with which he kills the Minotaur: the *labrys*, or double ax.[7]

But in the myth of the hero, what becomes of Ariadne? In one version, she is slain by Artemis, while in another she is abandoned on the island of Naxos and then married to Dionysus. These myths mirror the very process of "hybridization," for the first is about the supersession of the Goddess by a goddess of the new pantheon, while the other is about her absorption into the myth of a god who takes over many of her attributes. Ariadne's empowerment of the hero, an act that legitimizes and solidifies his status, is the mythic equivalent of the Lion's Gate, where the sacred pillars and the lions protect a male bastion. At other times, though, the strength of the hero in the new order is set in opposition to the old order of the Goddess, nowhere more clearly than in Homer's *Odyssey*.

In this epic quest for the heroic identity, Odysseus has Athena as his Olympian advocate, although their relationship differs markedly from that of Ariadne and Theseus. Throughout the poem, Athena "reinforces his strengths but only after he has proven himself capable of survival without her aid."[8] She helps him but ultimately does not empower him. Athena was probably Mycenaean in origin, a transformation of the Minoan Goddess. Like her, Athena has her epiphany in the bird, and is associated with the snake. In the change, though, from the ethos of Minoan Crete to that of Mycenae, the Goddess of the Household becomes the goddess of war.[9] While she is still associated with fertility (she endows Greece with the olive tree), Athena is no longer born of woman or earth but springs full-blown from Zeus' head after he has swallowed her mother, Metis. This myth, in fact, aptly describes one aspect of what happens to the Goddess in the Greek pantheon. Athena is, as the *Odyssey* shows, a goddess of heroic aspect whose strengths mirror those of her mortal protégé, Odysseus.

The deep opposition between the new heroic world and the world of the Goddess is demonstrated by the nature of the obstacles that impede Odysseus' return to Ithaca. While throughout the epic his great enemy is Poseidon, the god of the violent sea, Poseidon is less Olympian than chthonic. His epithets in the poem, "earth holder" and "earth shaker," remind us of his connections to the Goddess, as does his name, which means "spouse of De," or earth.[10] Calypso lives in a cave on a faraway island, set in a wave-tossed sea, and Homer's description of the cave, surrounded by a grove of trees and birds of all manner, its mouth encircled by a vine with clusters of grapes, draws on familiar symbols of the Goddess. In her speech to Hermes pleading to be permitted to marry Odysseus, Calypso identifies herself with Demeter, the Greek goddess of the earth's fertility, and specifically with her liaison with Iason, which later became part of the rites at Eleusis. Calypso, whose name means "engulf" or "conceal,"[11] is a primary threat to Odysseus and his pursuit of his heroic identity, and lest we think that her connection to the Goddess is incidental, we need only look at what she gives Odysseus as he leaves her:

> a great ax that was fitted to his palms and headed
> With bronze, with a double edge each way, and fitted inside it
> A very beautiful handle of olive wood, well hafted.[12]

In this great poem of the patriarchy, after relinquishing her hold on him Calypso as the Goddess arms the hero with her own emblem, the double ax. Long a symbol of and place of rebirth, the Goddess' cave-womb has become the place of oblivion for the heroic ideal; even though Calypso offers Odysseus immortality in exchange for staying with her, the hero must leave to save his identity.

Circe the enchantress also takes on a familiar aspect; surrounded by fawning lions and wolves, she is the Mistress of the Animals as seen through patriarchal eyes: her beasts are only frightening in their external aspect, since they have been denatured. She transforms Odysseus' men into pigs, an animal sacred to the Goddess in the Neolithic and the sacrificial animal at the peak sanctuary of the Goddess at Mount Jouctas and elsewhere. She is femininity incarnate in all of its destructive aspects, until the hero, fortified by a drug that renders him immune to her spells, threatens her in return. With the hero's challenge, she becomes the feminine controlled, and on these terms Odysseus can sleep with her. Like Calypso, she is associated with death and the chthonic, for she tells the hero the way to the underworld.

Symbolism long associated with the Goddess, especially that of the sacred cave, is used in the epic to give nuance to the pursuit of the heroic identity. In the nineteenth book of the *Odyssey*, Odysseus, disguised as a wanderer from Crete, tells his wife, Penelope, that he encountered her husband there. Odysseus pretends he is a grandson of the legendary Minos, son of Zeus, and that he entertained Odysseus, who had been washed up at the cave of Eileithyia on his way to Troy, narrowly escaping storm winds. This is once again an unmistakable reference to the nature of Odysseus' obstacles, the ethos of the Goddess, but it also connects the mythic cave of childbirth with the other caves in the

The Citadel at Mycenae

poem, those of Calypso and Polyphemus, the Cyclops, son of Poseidon, whom Odysseus blinds. Every cave in the epic stands in opposition to the birth of the heroic self; even the sacred site of the goddess of childbirth offers nothing but death and oblivion.

In Homer's telling, the island of the Cyclops is extraordinarily fertile, requiring no effort for the yielding of its fruits ("But all growed for them, without seed planting, without cultivation"); its lawless denizens live, moreover, in "caverns hollowed among the peaks of the high mountains." The island has been traditionally assumed to be Sicily, another island where the Goddess was honored and whose waters were roiled in myth by Scylla and

Charybdis, two other monstrous threats to the heroic journey. It is an island that could have been a great power if the Cyclopes had had ships, since it was not only fertile but full of wild goats and possessed of easy harbors. Homer's description of Polyphemus as a "peak of the high mountains standing away from the others" presents the danger he holds for the hero in terms of the sacred symbol of the Goddess, a mythic iconography that makes clear the conflict between the old and new orders, as well as among the mythic islands, the sea, and the heroic ideal. In Polyphemus, as she is in the figure of the Minotaur, the Goddess as nature is degraded to the monstrous. By blinding Polyphemus in his cave, Odysseus may go from being "Nobody" to claiming his own identity, a hero born through violence in what had once been the sacred womb of the Goddess.

And so the culture of Old Europe, the religion of the Goddess, and their sacred iconography are by turns absorbed, transformed, and negated by the religion of the sky god Zeus and the heroic ideal of the warrior kings. The sacred landscape of the Goddess as realized on Crete and elsewhere provides the framework of meaning for the new order of the Greeks and their temples, as Vincent Scully has demonstrated: the older sacred places symbolically empower the new edifices, as the Goddess in various forms empowers the new warriors. Yet the essential ideological and spiritual opposition of the Goddess and the sky god survives. With the reformulation of deity comes the redefinition of humankind. And we need only look at the familiar myth of Pandora, who was created on the authority of Zeus to punish Prometheus for stealing fire from the heavens and giving it to humanity, to grasp some of what the act of redefining implies. Pandora's name means "all gifts," a reflection not only of the various gifts of life, charm, and beauty bestowed upon her by the gods and the goddesses but of her ancestry in the Goddess, who is indeed the source of all gifts; as Jane Harrison has shown, the iconographic depiction of Pandora consistently derives from the familiar depiction of the Goddess as the all-giving earth.[13] But in the looking glass of the sky god, Pandora is the creatrix of death and pestilence, the female responsible for all evil.

Greek Vase Showing Ariadne, Theseus, and the Minotaur

She hands him the thread, thus assuring his triumph over the Minotaur, the monster of what was once the Goddess' precinct. Although in this depiction Theseus holds a simple sword, elsewhere his weapon is the double ax, or *labrys*.

9 The Legacy of the Goddess: Greece

The search for the Goddess in the civilization that becomes classical Greece involves looking for the underlying relationship between the old order and the new. As we began to see in Homeric myth, that relationship is contradictory and complex: sometimes the old order provides the symbolic and spiritual foundation for the new; other times, the two orders persist in perpetual conflict. In the written record of Greece's civilization, with Plato its most articulate spokesman and reflected in the lines and proportions of sacred architecture as well, the Goddess of the old order is no longer present. The classical Greek world liked to present itself as totally new, self-invented, and thoroughly distinct from what came before. But the future always partakes of the past, no matter how fervently its participants wish to be modern.

Eleusis was classical Greece's existential, just as Delphi was its spiritual, *omphalos.* Eleusis' site had been sacred for two thousand years before the Age of Pericles, and it is not surprising that its location reflects the sacred landscape of the Goddess. Nestled on a rocky ridge at the corner of the then verdant and fertile Thriasian Plain, close to the waters of the Bay of Eleusis, the site is bounded by mountains and hills on three sides and water on the other. Mount Kithairon and Mount Parnes close the plain on the north, while the horned mountain Kerata (so named because its peaks resemble the horns of an animal) closes it on the southwest.[1] But it is Eleusis' mythological and symbolic landscape that resonates with deeper meaning.

Eleusis was the site of the Great Mysteries, the destination of a procession that began in Athens some fourteen miles away and ended in rites of initiation at the Telestrion. At the core of these rites are two goddesses, Demeter and Persephone, mother and daughter, both of whom are closely connected to the Goddess. The legacy of the Goddess is embedded not only in the goddesses but also in the sacred architecture and the spiritual meaning of the rituals themselves: Eleusis' ties to the great Goddess and the rites of the Neolithic coexisted, albeit incongruously, with Greek classicism and beyond. Precisely what happened in these rites is unknown since the initiates were forbidden on pain of death to speak of them. Through the silence of the ages, details may be gleaned from the parody contained in Aristophanes' comedy *The Frogs,* but far more important are the voices that impart a sense of wonder, that speak of the transformation experienced by the initiates and of their spiritual reconciliation with life and death. We begin with their reverence so that we may somehow recapture the communion that Eleusis offered.

From Isocrates, the orator who was Plato's contemporary, we learn that the sacred Mysteries "fortify the initiated against all the terrors of death, and inspire them with the

Demeter and Kore

In the myth of the mother and daughter, here depicted on a funerary stele, aspects of the Goddess as life-giver and source of the fruits of the earth (Demeter) and source of death (Kore or Persephone), as Mother and Maiden, are split in two separate, yet linked, personages.

pleasing hopes of a happy immortality."[2] More than 250 years later, the Roman Cicero focuses on transformation and learning: "For by their means we have been brought out of our barbarous and savage mode of life and educated and refined to a state of civilization; and as the rites are called 'initiations,' so in very truth we have learned from them the beginnings of life, and have gained the power not only to live happily, but also to die with a better hope."[3] And a century after Cicero, the flame of Eleusis still flickered brightly with mystery for the Roman Seneca: "Some sacred things are not revealed once and for all. Eleusis always keeps in reserve something to show to those who revisit. Nature does not reveal her mysteries once and for all. We believe we are her initiates, but we are only hanging around the forecourt."[4]

At the center of the Eleusinian rites lies a myth of mother and daughter, recounted in the seventh century B.C. Homeric hymn to Demeter.[5] Its subject is death and rebirth, the focus of the rites celebrated at Eleusis; even the name *Eleusis*, believed by the ancients to mean "passage" or "gate," suggests that both the place and the rites are "the passage between two worlds," those of life and death.[6] It may be too that the non-Greek word *Eleusis* is connected etymologically to *Eileithyia*, the goddess of childbirth.[7]

Kore, the maiden (sometimes known as Persephone), daughter of Demeter, is gathering flowers in a field when she is tempted by the sight of a narcissus; the flower is a trap set by Gaia on Zeus' orders, and when Kore picks it, the earth opens up and Plouton (the "wealthy one"), god of the underworld, snatches and rapes her. Only Hecate, a daughter of Rhea, and Helios, god of the sun, hear Kore's cries. For nine days, Demeter wanders the earth searching for her daughter, carrying blazing torches and neither eating nor drinking nor washing; no god or mortal comes to her aid. On the tenth day, Hecate and Helios finally come forth, and Demeter flees Olympus in anger and wanders the earth unrecognized until she comes to the home of the king of Eleusis, Keleos. Disguised as an old woman, she sits beneath an olive tree, unnoticed, until the daughters of the king greet her and invite her home with them. There, Demeter tells them that her name is Doso and that she has been brought by force from Crete by pirates — a pattern of heritage familiar to us from other myths for endowing a member of the pantheon with the Goddess' roots. The daughters introduce her to their mother, Metaneira, who had borne a much-loved son late in life. Demeter refuses all wine and food but bids them to prepare a potion for her, a *kykeon* of barley and water. Metaneira invites the disguised Demeter to become her son's nurse, and under her care the boy thrives, fed ambrosia by the goddess and hidden in the fire at night to grant him the immortality that is the provenance of the gods. Metaneira,

Ruins of the Telestrion, Eleusis

though, is curious about the child's growth and keeps a watch on the new nurse; horrified, she discovers the child in the fire at night. It is then that Demeter reveals herself and her true form, decrying Metaneira's human shortsightedness, which has denied her son's immortality. Demeter instructs the people of Eleusis to build her a temple with an altar beneath it, on the ridge that juts forth, saying that she will instruct them in her rites.

A temple is built, and Demeter, still mourning the loss of Kore, withdraws to it. In her anger and grief she renders the world fallow so that humanity can no longer live or sacrifice to the gods. Zeus is forced to call for her, and the other gods implore her to stop, but she refuses to let fruit grow on the earth until she has seen her daughter.

A compromise is reached: Kore may return if she has not eaten in the underworld. Plouton, though, has tricked her into eating the seed of the pomegranate, so that Kore cannot fully return. Instead, she is to spend one-third of the year in the underworld, and the rest above.

At its simplest level, the myth is about the cycles of vegetation and fertility, and the rites of Eleusis surely included some offering of first fruits to Demeter, who, like the Goddess of Crete, is the goddess of grain in full fruition, while her daughter represents the seed not yet flowered.[8] On another level, though, Demeter and Kore represent aspects of the life cycle in a single being, as do the other women in the myth. Demeter and Kore are mother and maiden, two stages in a woman's life; in disguise, Demeter takes on the appearance of an old woman, "one who is beyond childbearing and the gifts of Aphrodite," thus completing the cycle from maiden to mother to crone, the cycle of the Goddess herself. Yet even in Demeter's aspect of crone, her motherliness is evident, though in marked contrast to that of Metaneira, the mortal mother. The figure of Rhea or Gaia reminds us that the Goddess was the source of life and death, for here Gaia is both the source of the loss of Kore (in the narcissus) and the source of rebirth, since she brings Demeter the news of Zeus' compromise and orders Demeter to return the fruits of life to humanity. At Eleusis what was once the sacred unity of the Goddess becomes the duality of Demeter and Kore. And the myth is not simply about the breaking of the immortal cycle, as a daughter of a goddess is abducted in death, but about confrontation with death. Faced with her own child's death, Demeter, the Mother, tries unsuccessfully to make a mortal child immortal.

The sacred precinct of Eleusis and its rites reflect and reverberate with the meanings inherent in the myth. Within the sacred precinct, not surprisingly, is a cave; possibly it is an early sanctuary of the Goddess, but after the Dorian invasion and in the context of the Demeter-Kore myth it becomes the precinct of Plouton and the symbolic entrance to the underworld. We know that the earliest structure on the hillock of Eleusis was a Mycenaean megaron, a building of a single chamber, which was later enlarged to include

The Erechthion on the Acropolis (421–406 B.C.)

The structure was built to house the city's sacred tokens (Athena's olive tree and Poseidon's trident, among them). Here, the Goddess as pillar is reduced to decorative element.

three additional rooms.[9] The first tiny shrine faced east (as did the later Telestrion, which replaced it) and the pass at Daphni through which the procession from Athens flowed.[10] The megaron may have performed the same functions in the first rites at Eleusis as did the Telestrion in the later versions of the rituals. The hymn to Demeter refers to a "temple": in Greece, a building that housed a statue of the deity worshipped. The Telestrion, however, was not a temple, but a place built specifically for a congregation to participate in rites.

The design of the Telestrion itself is fascinating. As a building meant to accommodate several thousand people, its design seems at first oddly antithetical to its purposes. Through successive rebuildings, the plan remained essentially the same: a columned hall with windowless walls, punctuated by entrances. Koroibos, the architect of Eleusis from 446 to 440 B.C., built a vast square hall (about 170 feet in length and 180 feet in width), with its west section cut out of the living rock. Its forty-two columns, arranged in rows seven across and six long, divided its space.[11] Vincent Scully notes that "it seems clear that as many columns as possible were desired inside, in order to create an interior more labyrinthine, mysterious, and grovelike."[12] Within the Telestrion was a small room, perhaps echoing the form of the megaron, that held the *hiera,* or sacred objects of the Mysteries.

The celebration of the Mysteries began with the priesthood of Eleusis leading a procession to Athens; the *hiera* were carried in sacred cists (*kistai*) tied with red ribbons.[13] On the first day of celebration the initiates gathered together in Athens; on the second day they proceeded to the sea for rites of purification, carrying small pigs. The pigs were ceremonially cleansed in the waters and then sacrificed, reminiscent of the rites of the Goddess in Crete with the pig as her sacrificial animal; it suggests too that at least some of the ceremonies were chthonic rather than Olympian. The third day may have been a day of sacrifice, while the fourth was one of rest. On the fifth day, called Iacchos, the procession back to Eleusis began, the initiates specially clothed and crowned with myrtle. A wooden statue of Iacchos, bearing a torch and crowned with a wreath of myrtle, accompanied the procession of initiates, who sang and danced along the fourteen-mile Sacred Way, through the pass at Daphni, on to the Eleusinian Plain, circling the shore of the Gulf of Eleusis. In Vincent Scully's words, "Every step of this route is marked by the appearance, disappearance, and reappearance of the sacred landscape symbols," a pattern familiar to us from the sacred processions at Knossos under the sacred horns.[14] At Eleusis, the horns of Mount Kerata slide in and out of the procession's view, "the mystic object found and lost."[15]

The processional journey was symbolic, which was made clear by the practice at the bridge over the Eleusinian Kephisos, the water that must be crossed before the Sacred Way yields to the outer court of the Sanctuary. On the bridge, men hurled insults and taunts at the initiates, who did not retort, a symbolic stripping away of self that has its analogies in other rites of initiation.[16] Thus prepared, the initiates entered the Sanctuary.

The Sanctuary itself, bounded by high walls, was the locale of the secret parts of the Mysteries, and comprises a symbolic landscape that reflects the myth. Approaching the Sanctuary's gates, bearing their torches, the initiates would dance by the Kallichoron well, where Demeter sat, dancing in celebration of their first vision of the goddess. The next day they would rest and fast, purifying themselves as Demeter had done after the loss of Kore. They may have drunk barley and water, the *kykeon,* as Demeter had done. Then perhaps they stood on the step of the terrace by the Sacred Way before the Mirthless Stone, where the goddess had mourned. They probably imitated the goddess' search for Kore on the terrace of the temple, and then gathered with their torches still blazing at the cave of Plouton, symbolic entrance to the underworld, both to experience Kore's death and to anticipate her rebirth. Through the landscape of the Sanctuary, the known myth acquired greater and deeper experiential meaning. They would then have made their way in the darkness to the Telestrion, where the light from their torches would have flickered eerily among the columns, just as the torches of their ancestors once flickered among the stalactites and stalagmites of the sacred caves. Then, echoing Vincent Scully's description of Minoan ritual, "the participant was drawn at last into the cavern and enclosed by the goddess' pillared shrine."[17] Since the Telestrion had no seats but a bank of steps around its interior walls, the initiates might have stood upon them, pushing against one another until, in Vincent Scully's re-creation, they flowed out among the columns, perhaps part of a sacred serpentine dance.

Protected by a silence kept through the centuries, the form the revelation at Eleusis actually took remains shrouded. There were probably three elements of ceremony: the *dromena,* that which was enacted; the *legomena,* that which was spoken; the *deiknymena,* the sacred objects that were shown. The *dromena* may have been a dramatic presentation of the central myth, or of the journey to the underworld, or of a sacred marriage. Mircea Eliade has suggested that before the rebirth of revelation, some form of symbolic death may have taken place, corroborated by the Greek wordplay on "initiation" (*teleisthai*) and "dying" (*teleutan*).[18] The *legomena* may have been composed of the reading of a sacred text or simply incantatory words or verses.

It is the *hiera,* though, the sacred objects that are the final source of revelation, that are most mysterious and intriguing, and that have been the subject of centuries of scholarly debate. Since they make up the secret heart of the ceremonies, we know the least about them. Clement of Alexandria, hardly an impartial commentator, leaves us a tantalizing list of sacred objects that resonate with the symbolism of the old Goddess: cakes, a serpent, pomegranates, leaves and stalks, poppies, and a model of the vulva.[19] If these were indeed the contents of the sacred chests, or *kistai,* then the legacy of Minoan religion is clear, for they combine the themes of death (in the serpent and the poppies) with those of rebirth (the pomegranate, symbol of the womb in color and seed; the stalk and the leaves; the sacred triangle itself) in a familiar iconographic language. Hippolytus of Rome gives another familiar image, a single harvested spray of wheat, reaped with a stone ax, symbol (as is the pomegranate) of the one and the many, of the life cycle of all on earth, of the Goddess herself.[20] More prosaically, George Mylonas has suggested that the *kistai* contained Mycenaean relics, handed down through the generations — perhaps images of the Goddess herself.[21]

Finally, after the revelation of the *kistai,* and perhaps daylight or the light of a fire streaming through the clerestory of the Telestrion, the initiates were transformed, possessed of a knowledge that eased both the living of life and the acceptance of death. The Telestrion takes us back in time to the labyrinthine, symbolic structures of Malta, Ireland, and Crete. So does the larger sacred precinct of Eleusis, with its cave, terraces, and buildings carved out of living rock. So does the mirroring of the inner journey of the initiate in the external landscape. Behind the bright spiritual torch of classical Greece flickers an older flame, that of the Goddess, whose spirit provided part of the illumination that was, for thousands of years, Eleusis.

Under the watchful eye of Zeus, chief god of the Olympians, Delphi, sanctuary of Apollo's oracle and spiritual center of all ancient Greece, appears to be an emblem of the triumph of the Olympian pantheon and of the victory of Apollo's intellect and civilized purity over the darker forces of birth and death that belonged to the Goddess. To the Greeks, Delphi was the *omphalos* (navel) or center of the world, said to have been established by Zeus when he let fly two eagles from the extremes of the earth. Here resided the power and the prophecy of Apollo, the sacred communication between gods and men. But both history and the site itself tell a different story, one that further illustrates the complexity of the change from the old order of the Goddess.

The sacredness of the site is a legacy of the earth goddess Ge, or Gaia, who was worshipped here through Mycenaean times, until the Dorians arrived in 1100 B.C. Beneath the cella of Apollo's temple, excavators found part of a Minoan rhyton in the shape of a lioness head, similar to one found at Knossos, as well as Mycenaean figurines of the Goddess. These items suggest that indeed there is a historical connection, partly preserved in myth, between worship at Knossos and the earliest rites at Delphi.[22] The Greeks

Delphi

Caves, water, and the
shining peaks of the
Phaeriades combine to
make this precinct sacred.

The Temple of Apollo, Delphi

connected the name of this sacred place with *delphys,* or "womb."[23] Myth tells us that Gaia first uttered prophecies in a rock-cleft cave, guarded by her son, the serpent Pytho. Young Apollo, son of Zeus and the mortal Leto, killed the snake, ancient symbol of the Goddess' female power, and left Delphi to purify himself, only to return and claim the oracle as his own. Aeschylus in *The Eumenides* reminds his audience of the ancient order of succession with the words "I first give honor in my prayer to her / who of the gods first prophesied the Earth," and the extreme violence of this mythic confrontation reverberates throughout the play. When the female Furies, symbolizing and speaking for the Goddess' dominion, castigate Apollo for desecrating the *omphalos,* they make the mythic meaning explicit:

The very stone centre of earth here in our eyes horrible
with blood and curse stands plain to see.

Himself divine, he has spoiled his secret shrine's
hearth with the stain, driven and hallooed the action on.
He made man's way cross the place of the ways of god
and blighted age-old distributions of power.[24]

Delphi abounds with the landscape symbols of the Goddess. Nestled in a rugged cleft of
Mount Parnassos, it is bounded by the steep undercliffs of the mountain on the north (the
Phaeriades, or "Shining Rocks," home to eagles and vultures), by ridges on the east and
west, and by Mount Cirphis on the south. It is set into the earth and enveloped by it.
Between the two mountains, the river Pleistos flows, snaking its way through the landscape, while the Castalian spring rises and flows down from a deep gorge in the center of
the Parnassian cliff. Vincent Scully has pointed out that the landscape of Delphi resounds
with other, darker meanings as well: it was shaken by earthquakes, its features were
transformed by rock falls and landslides, and it was subject to violent changes in light and
dark, both from the shadows of the peaks and the passing of thunderclouds overhead,
and the brilliance of the falling Castalian waters.[25] The site resounds with the power of
the Goddess in both her life-giving and chthonic aspects — in the luminous cascade of
the water, the dark crevices of the earth, in the power of life-giving Gaia and the words
that issue as though from the womb of the earth. But it also must have seemed, as Scully
points out, to be "the place where the conflict between the old way, that of the goddess of
the earth, and the new way, that of men and their Olympian gods, was most violently
manifest."[26]

Although Apollo supplanted Gaia and took the oracles as his own, Delphi reminds
us that he did not entirely eclipse her. The sanctuary of Athena Pronaia (*pronaia* means
"before the shrine") lies below Apollo's sanctuary under the cliffs, and might well have
been visited first in ancient times before one climbed the steep way to Apollo's domain.
The position of the sanctuary symbolizes Athena's role as the protector of the place (as
Polias) but also serves to restore certain aspects of the old Goddess' power to the sacred
landscape, to mitigate the change wrought by the violence of the Olympian assault. Athena
too is symbolized by the snake, thus repairing at least part of Gaia's power snatched by
Apollo. Sacred legend reminded visitors to this holy place of the ancient order of things,
of the Mycenaean ruins that lie below the Temple of Apollo's floor. In another myth of
succession, this one decidedly less violent than the slaying of the sacred snake, the Homeric

hymn to the Pythian Apollo tells how the god, taking on the shape of a dolphin, jumped upon a ship carrying Cretans from Knossos and took the vessel to the harbor nearest to Delphi. Reverting to his real shape, Apollo then ordered the Cretans to become servants in his temple, thus endowing him and his precinct with the power of the sacred Cretan roots of the Goddess. Finally, though, it is the land itself, the original inspiration for humankind's sanctified place, that makes the power of the Goddess shine through the Olympian fabric. The great Apollo's sanctuary still lies enveloped by the shadows of the peaks, in the clefts of the earth.

The physical violence at Delphi, of earthquake and falling rock, shadow and thunderstorm, permeated its rites and rituals from its ancient beginnings as a sanctuary of Ge to Apollonian times. At Delphi the oracular power was invested in the place and came from deep within the earth itself. The source of its holy prophesies was not, as was practiced elsewhere, the observation of the flight of birds or the entrails of a sacrificed animal. It was instead the frenzied ecstasy of a priestess who inhaled the mystic but foul-smelling vapors of the earth itself that came up through the cleft (the *chasma*) in the temple's floor, drank of the sacred spring's waters, clenched Apollo's laurel leaf between her lips, and was literally possessed by his divine intelligence.[27] Tradition held that she descended into a cavern or corridor (the *adyton*); within the *adyton* was the *omphalos*, the sacred stone the Furies in *The Eumenides* accuse Apollo of desecrating. Jane Harrison has identified the *omphalos* as not merely a carved stone but a stone carved in the form of a tumulus or grave mound, the grave mound of Gaia's sacred snake;[28] Sir Arthur Evans, the excavator of Knossos, connected the *omphalos* with the sacred stalagmites in the caves of Crete, particularly that of Eileithyia.[29] Dressed in white with a gold headdress, the Pythia of Apollo sat on a tripod over the *chasma*, a live serpent coiled around its base. Heiress, in fifth-century Greece, to the Minoan Snake Goddess and to the sibyls who sat in the caves at Delphi before her, she was inspired by the earth's breath, empowered by the *omphalos* of Gaia's snake, uttering the words that connected the darker domain of the Goddess with that of humankind. Even the name Pythia summons up the connection between the old order and the new: *Pythia* derives from *pythein*, or "rotting," a reference to the rotting corpse of the snake which makes the sanctuary Apollo's.

We know from ancient accounts that upon entering the classical edifice that now surrounded the oracle, the suppliant would first have seen the words "Know Thyself" and "Nothing to Excess," strictures to reassure him of the order of civilization for which Apollo and Greece stood. (Dionysus, a reminder of the darker side of nature, also was worshipped at Delphi, but it was Apollo who prevailed.) In marked contrast to these mottoes, however, there remained the violent and exhausting writhing of the priestess who sat before the

Tholos, Sanctuary of Athena Pronaia (c. Mid-Fourth Century B.C.)

The ancient association of the Goddess and the circle carries with it echoes of prehistory, the concentric patterns of earlier ages, the configurations of menhirs and stones, the roundness of the female body, the swell of pregnancy, and the shrines of the chthonic Goddess. Built on Gaia's sacred ground, the Tholos is a radial circle with an exterior ring of Doric columns and an interior of Corinthian columns (one of the earliest uses of the Corinthian). With their leaves spreading over the capitals, rising within the darkness of the inner chamber, the tree-like shapes, familiar from Minoan architecture and elsewhere, evoke the Earth Goddess and her power. The circular shape of the temple, unlike the other buildings of the site, does not orient the eye to a specific point in the landscape but, instead, forces it to take in the multiplicity of earth shapes that surround it, the primal domain of the Goddess.

Sanctuary of Hera (Heraion), Samos

Samos is a large island off the west coast of Asia Minor. It was on Samos that Hera was said to renew her virginity by bathing in the Imbrasos, an annual event of ritual celebration. The earliest ruins on Samos are Mycenaean, and from the tenth century B.C. onward, a stone altar stood at the center of the sacred precinct. The altar was later enlarged and elaborated, and survived until Roman times as the focal point of the sanctuary.

The first temple of Hera was built in the eighth century but replaced within the next one hundred years. In the sixth century B.C. the sanctuary was totally rebuilt with a new temple, which was then destroyed by fire. The replacement temple was planned as the largest temple in Greece but was never completed.

The processional routes leading to the sacred site were lined with tributes, among them the exquisite statue of Hera now in the Louvre (p. 184).

Statue of Hera from Samos
(c. 570 B.C.)

The delicately modeled
draperies reveal the feminine
form of Hera's body. Stately
and self-possessed, this vision
of Hera is far removed from
the jealous wife preserved
in myth.

184

suppliant, her seizures framed against the starkness of marble, and the coiling and recoiling of the mantic snake at her feet.

Her agonies were evident, though what she voiced were probably no more than incoherent murmurs, left to be interpreted by the Prophet and the Holy Ones, members of the leading Delphic families who surrounded the tripod and received her suppliant's questions in writing beforehand. It should not surprise us that the violent energy of the Goddess still lingers in this Apollonian realm of classical proportions. The snake curled around the tripod reminds us of the snakes entwined on the body of the Cretan Goddess, emblems of her power over the underworld and the spirits of the dead. Like the Goddess, the snake encompasses the forces of both regeneration and death. While the shedding of her skin signifies rebirth, in her speed, cunning, and the venom of her bite is death.

The Pythia's ecstasy, her "divine madness," as Plato called it, reminds us of the Oracle Room at Malta, where voices of prophecy echoed through the womb-shaped rooms, and of the practice of divination through dream incubation. We are reminded too of the axes thrust into the clefts of the earth to release its divine power, high on the peaks in Crete. But unlike those earlier civilizations, here the Goddess has been subjugated, if not eradicated, by male rule. Two cultures and the irreconcilable ways of looking at life have been reduced and melded into a single myth. But it must be remembered that Apollo gained the power by slaying Ge's serpent, and that he, like Zeus before him, was empowered by the Goddess through his Cretan roots.

But in Apollo's Delphic sanctuary, the ancient power of the snake belongs to *him*. Even though it is a woman who serves as the organ to voice the utterances of the male divinity, the Pythia was either a maiden or a woman over the age of fifty dressed as a maiden, a female before or beyond her life-bearing capacities, removed in any case from the eternal fecundity of the Goddess. Although Athena guards the Apollonian shrine, preserving some of the Goddess' power in her symbolic snake and owl, she is armed and helmeted. More important, the classical Athena was born not of woman or even of the earth but sprang full-blown from Zeus' head.

Even if the Goddess had been tamed by the fifth century, and her shrines taken over and her powers distributed and transmuted, the conflict between her old order and the new lives on in this sacred site. Mircea Eliade reminds us that while "the supreme Apollonian lesson is expressed in the famous Delphic formula, 'Know thyself!'" and that "Apollonian serenity becomes, for the Greek, the emblem of spiritual perfection and hence of the spirit," discovery of spirit follows conflict and resolution and the mastery of "ecstatic and oracular techniques."[30] The prophecies that issue from the cleft in the earth belong in part to the old order, that of the Goddess of the sacred caves, and adulterate the Apollonian ideal. In the fifth century, Thucydides inveighed against this intrusion from another time, while Sophocles in his *Oedipus* cycle gave the conflict between the old order, represented by the Furies as well as the Delphic oracle, and the new, represented by the self-made man Oedipus, a powerful vitality.

So at Delphi the struggle continues, in the dark and primal force captured between those classical walls and in an ecstatic ritual inherited from another time.

Aspects of the Goddess were passed into the Greek Olympian pantheon in the figures of other goddesses (and some gods) because of tradition and because those aspects of the Goddess continued to address and express human needs. These Olympian goddesses were part of the patriarchal family Zeus ruled, a family full of discord, rebellion, and infidelity, familiar in a very human way; the divine wife and daughters were subordinate to the final authority of the patriarch.[31] Although they lost their dignity in the overarching hierarchy, locally, usually in places and on sites with Neolithic and Mycenaean roots, the goddesses took on the aspect of the old in their solemnity and independence.

So, while Hera is the beleaguered jealous wife of myth, nonetheless in worship she takes on aspects of the Goddess. Like the Goddess, she is parthenogenetic: of her four children, one, Hephaestos, is born of her alone. Her name, which probably means simply "our lady," also reveals her ancestry. Vincent Scully has demonstrated that her sanctuaries at Perachora, Samos, and Argos identify her as the mother of the earth, as well as connecting her to Eileithyia, although only in the context of marriage.[32] At Argos, like Samos, thought to be the place of her birth, it was said that Zeus came to her in the form of a cuckoo and wooed her and thus brought her under his dominion; the bird was held sacred to her. She was first worshipped in the form of a pillar at Argos, like the Minoan Goddess before her; Scully suggests, too, that the addition of an enclosed building at Argos (built after the first temple burned in 423 B.C.) might indicate "a continuance or revival of the rites of the old goddess inside."[33] A chryselephantine statue of Hera made by Polyclitus after 423 B.C. depicted her as crowned and enthroned, with a scepter in one hand and a pomegranate, symbol of female fertility, in the other. The first oxen used in plowing were dedicated to Hera by the Argives, while the sprouting ears of corn were called "the flowers of Hera," indicating her connection to earth and its fruits. She was worshipped, too, as the goddess of flowers, and girls who served in her temples were known as "flower-bearers."

Rites elsewhere not only celebrated the marriage between Hera and Zeus, but, more important, Hera alone. Like the Goddess before her, she symbolized the earth's cycles,

Hera Eileithyia, from the Heraion at the Mouth of the Sele

Naked, the goddess kneels in the act of childbirth. The dove in her hand symbolizes fertility.

OVERLEAF: **Temple of Hera II (Formerly the Temple of Neptune), Paestum**

187

life's stages, and by extension, those of her female worshippers. Among her titles were "maiden," "wife," and "widow," and the Argives, according to Pausanias, believed that Hera recovered her virginity each year by bathing in a spring: the eternal cycle renewed.

The Heraion at Paestum (its Roman name; its Greek name was Poseidonia), though, is unique, since it represents a Greek sacred precinct in foreign surroundings, in southern Campania in the south of Italy. The Greeks came to the area sometime in the first half of the seventh century and established their first sanctuary to Hera at Sybaris, at the mouth of the river Sele. The location points to primacy of agricultural concerns for the settlers; Sybaris and Paestum have no port, and the first sanctuary faces inland. Hera was worshipped here in her aspect of earth goddess, and her sacred place overlooking the valley expressed "a will to command the land and to bring what must have seemed to the Greeks its miraculously wide expanse under the eye of their own goddess and under the eyes of the worshippers at her shrine."[34] The earliest statues show Hera with a child in one arm and a pomegranate in the other.[35]

During the sixth and fifth centuries B.C., the settlement flourished, and new monuments were raised to honor the goddess whom local festivals celebrated. A statue from the second half of the sixth century showing a circle of dancers with their arms raised confirms the connections between the worship of Hera and the old ways of the Goddess in Crete. The newer temples are no longer at the mouth of the river but form a part of an ambitious plan for the city of Paestum, which had at its center a religious and civic area flanked by two residential districts, a sacred rectangle within. At one end of the rectangle stood two temples of Hera, Hera I, built about 550 B.C. (formerly known as the Basilica) and Hera II, built around 450 B.C. (formerly known as the Temple of Neptune). At the end stood a temple of Athena.

Both temples face a conical hill with clefts (as do the other sites of Hera) — the Greek sacred landscape, inherited from the Minoans, brought to foreign soil. At Paestum, excavators found thousands of votive offerings to the goddess (thirty thousand in one pit alone), showing Hera as Eileithyia, in addition to figurines of doves, pomegranates, worshippers bearing geese, and pregnant women.[36]

Artemis, too, inherited aspects of the Goddess, most evident in her role as Mistress of the Wild Animals. She is the goddess of wild nature, unspoiled by man. Her symbolic animals, the lion and the bear, have roots that go back to the Paleolithic: a lioness and her cub are engraved at the sacred cave of Les Trois Frères in France, while, closer in time, the Goddess of the Mountains at Knossos had guardian lions by her side. The bear in the iconography of Old Europe is associated with motherhood, water, and life,[37] and Artemis too was the goddess of fertility in man and animals, though not of the fields.[38] She helps women alone through the pain of labor and childbirth (as opposed to Hera, who protects in the context of marriage) and so also is called Eileithyia, but, like the wilderness she protects, she is a virgin. She is

> the great mother who resolutely avoids marriage as Hera could not avoid
> it, and who thereby remains free of domination by males and their law.
> Thus she protects the wild from rape by men, and her sites in Greece are
> haunted by that watchful, dangerous presence. She is everywhere in
> the untended lands.[39]

Not surprisingly, Artemis' sites of worship, near the mountains, shores, and swamps, are wilder than those of the other goddesses and gods.

The sanctuary of Artemis at Brauron lies at the foot of a little hill, not far from the

Temple of Athena (Formerly the Temple of Ceres), Paestum

As Vincent Scully notes, the very site of this temple, in contrast to the two temples of Hera, distinguishes Athena from Hera. While Hera is the legatee of the Goddess in her earthbound aspects, Athena here is the protectress of the city and civilization, her temple built on the highest ground, "raised above the landscape."

Temple of Hera I (Formerly the Basilica), Paestum

mouth of the marshy Erasinos River. Surrounded by hilly woodlands, full of wildlife, Brauron was occupied as early as the Neolithic and early Bronze Age. The oldest structure at Brauron was unearthed in a cavern that ran along the slope of the hill; within the cavern were four adjoining rooms on the north, reached by a parallel hallway on the south, which may have been the tomb of Iphigenia. The various myths pertaining to Iphigenia, the daughter of Agamemnon and Clytemnestra, point to the darker, chthonic side of this goddess of untamed nature. Agamemnon had offended Artemis by killing a stag in a grove sacred to her, and the goddess could be appeased only by the sacrifice of his daughter. There are various myths dealing with whether Iphigenia is actually sacrificed; in some, she is not and becomes a priestess of Artemis at Brauron, where she is eventually buried. Yet animal and perhaps human sacrifices continued to be associated with Artemis, and as Anne Baring and Jules Cashford note, "the goddess who personifies the wildness of nature evokes the most primitive fear of dependence on forces that are beyond the control of human beings, and whose law they can, therefore, violate without knowing it."[40]

Between the late sixth century and early fifth century B.C., a temple was erected at Brauron, one with a *pronoia,* a cella divided into three aisles by a double colonnade, and an *adyton,* a cavern or corridor. An altar may have stood east of the temple. At the western entrance to the cavern, a two-room sanctuary with an altar before it replaced the old megaron. From the northwest corner of the temple terrace, water gushed and was dammed into an artificial lake roughly triangular in shape. Artemis' ties to the Bear Goddess are articulated here, in a site that combines the sacred cave and the waters of life, both in their untamed form and in that of the sacred triangle. Women and young girls, unaccompanied by men, set forth for Brauron from Athens every fifth year to honor Artemis, protector of women and animals in childbirth. The site has two aspects, related but separated: the classical temple of the goddess, framed by a rounded hill across the valley, serene and beautiful; and the jagged edges of the cave, under the shadow of the temple.[41]

There, clad in their bearskins, little girls would form a procession and enter the megaron within the cave. Their path of emergence would have been between the rocks, a track that imitates the act of birth from the cavelike womb. Scully states that at Artemis' sanctuary "the cleft clearly celebrates the special and unsharable female act, when the bears, witnessed only by their goddess, drop their young in pain among the rocks, alone."[42]

Athena too shares the lineage of the Goddess, but she is the most transformed of all the Goddess' aspects; for the classical Greeks, she is the symbol of the achievement of Athens and Attica. Her symbols, the snake and the owl, make her origins evident, as does her name (simply *A Thea,* "a goddess"), although even as early as Mycenaean times, her Minoan roots had been overlaid by a new ethos, making her martial in spirit. Unlike the

Athena (Fifth Century B.C.)

A majestic maiden, this gilt and bronze Athena, found on the Acropolis, displays her heritage in the coiling snakes that decorate her peplos.

The Parthenon (447–438 B.C.)

other goddesses of the Greek pantheon whose beginnings in the Goddess remain visible, Athena's are largely symbolic. She is first and foremost the goddess of intelligence, as myth tells us: born out of Zeus' head, the seat of reason, her mother was Metis, goddess of intelligence. Protector of the hero and the heroic, she reminds us in Homer's *Odyssey* that among all the gods, she alone is famous for her intelligence (*metis*) and skill (XIII, 297). She is, in one sense, as far removed as possible from the chthonic aspect of the Goddess, the darker forces of nature. In Mircea Eliade's words, Athena represents "the sacrality of technical invention and the myth of intelligence";[43] she represents not only divine knowledge but also human wisdom. From her flow all of humanity's inventions. She is purity in spirit and mind, and on the Acropolis she was worshipped as Parthenos, the Virgin.

It is to the Acropolis, symbol of the greatness of Greece, that we finally turn, the still-point of the Eurocentric, patriarchal, intellectual universe. On this hill in 1200 B.C. stood a Mycenaean palace with sacred precincts and fortifications; the martial Athena was already here, surrounded by the Cyclopean barricade some five feet thick, the Pelasgic wall. From 520 B.C. forward, three or four temples preceded the Parthenon: the Old Temple of Athena and the Hekatompedon (literally the "hundred-foot temple"), which was surrounded by sculptures of Kouroi and Koria; the older Parthenon, or Pre-Parthenon, still unfinished; and all that surrounded it was destroyed by the Persians in 480 B.C.

It was Periclean Athens that rebuilt the sacred site, designed and constructed between 447 and 438 B.C. under the supervision of the sculptor Phidias and the architects Iktinos and Kallikrates. In the cella of the largest temple on the Greek mainland, its dimensions reflecting the size of the sacred object it was built to house, stood Phidias' great ivory and gold statue of Athena, rising forty feet in the air, helmeted and holding her shield and her sacred snake in her left hand, and a small Winged Victory in her right. The shield Athena held echoed the themes of the building's metopes: its inside was painted with the battle of the gods and the giants, and its outside carved with a battle of the Greeks and Amazons. The rim of the statue's sandals displayed a battle of the Greeks and the centaurs, echoed in the metopes as well. While the Maiden's House (that is, the Parthenon) retains the spatial orientation of the older sacred sites that preceded it, looking toward the horned peaks of Mount Hymettos, the Goddess at the peak has been overtaken by the harmony of classical proportion and geometric principle. The astonishing sculptures that decorated the Parthenon, long since dispersed among the museums of the world, also symbolized the victory of the mind, as embodied by Athena, over the forces of nature and chaos. On the east frieze of the building, the sacred procession and the presentation of the peplos of Athena was pictured in the presence of gods and goddesses of the pantheon: Hermes, Dionysus, Demeter, Ares, Hebe, Hera, and Zeus. The west frieze depicted the procession's departure.[44] The goddess' birth was celebrated on one pediment, with Athena and Zeus at the center: in Aeschylus' words from *The Eumenides,* "She who was never fostered in the dark of the womb / Yet such child as no goddess could bring to birth" (665–666). On the other pediment, Athena's triumph over Poseidon for control of Attica and Athens was depicted. Poseidon, like the earliest versions of Athena, had links to the chthonic Goddess: he was, like her, the source of earthquakes, and his name means "husband of earth."[45] In Homer's *Odyssey,* he stands opposed to the hero and the heroic and aligned with the obstacles preventing Odysseus' realization of self, while Athena is Odysseus' champion. While Poseidon provides humanity with the horse, Athena invents the bridle and chariot to harness and use its power; while Poseidon controls the sea, Athena teaches the craft of shipbuilding and the art of the rudder. In their competition, Poseidon's gift to Attica is the salt spring that comes of the earth, while Athena's is the cultivated olive tree, and with that, she conquers the husband of earth,[46] the ultimate triumph of the Olympian over the old chthonic powers. The metopes of the Parthenon echo the same theme: here are the victories of the Greeks over the Trojans and the Amazons, the Lapiths over the centaurs, symbols of "the Greek conquest of everything barbarous, of all monstrosity and grossness."[47] The Olympians, led by Athena on the Acropolis, symbolize "order, justice, and beauty," as the pediments of the temple show them not squabbling but in harmony. In the sight of the Parthenon, in its ordered universe of proportion, *man's* work of intelligence and creativity in celebration and invocation of the goddess, we are as far away from the sacred cave as *mankind* can take us. And so it is, then, that in Aeschylus' *The Eumenides,* which is set first at Delphi and later on the Acropolis before Athena's temple, Athena casts her vote for Orestes, saying, "I am always for the male / With all my heart, and strongly on my father's sides" (737–738), thus disenfranchising the Eumenides, emissaries of the old Goddess. She gives them a sacred precinct on the Acropolis, but transforms them from avenging chthonic spirits to kindly ones of the new order.

The last word, though, is Plato's, for in the famous allegory of the cave in his *Republic,* one of the intellectual cornerstones of Western, patriarchal civilization, the Goddess is finally shackled and constrained, and given a cultural context from which she has yet to be set free. The subject is truth, and Plato's choice of metaphor is extraordinary and deliberate. He asks us to imagine men in a cavernous chamber, with an entrance open to the light and a long passage running the width of the cave. The men have had their heads and legs shackled since early childhood and can see only what is in front of them. A fire burns behind them, throwing shadows on the wall of the cave. Plato asks that we imagine a procession of people on a parapet carrying carved objects in the shapes of humans and animals. The shadows of the objects are cast upon the cavern's walls, although not those of the people who carry them. He recounts how the reality of the prisoners would, in fact, be the shadows, not the objects, and how if one of the men were to be set free and advance toward the fire, the light of the blaze would temporarily blind him. And how, if he were forcibly dragged out of the cave, he would again be blinded, and in pain. His eyes could first bear only the light of the moon and the stars, and then the sun's reflection. Finally, he would be able to look at the sun directly, and at that moment "infer and conclude that this it is that provides the seasons and the courses of the year and presides over all things in the visible region. . . ."[48] And then, if he went back into the cave, once again the darkness would blind his eyes. And if he tried to set the other prisoners free and lead them into the light, they would kill him.

Surely what Plato draws upon in his allegory, as his contemporaries would be quick to understand, are the ancient rites of the Goddess, held in her sacred precincts and inherited from Knossos and Mycenae, still part of the Greek spiritual landscape. Her ancient truths become in the allegory mere shadows of reality, her processional a puppet show of figurines and animals. Her precinct is the prison of the mind and spirit that men are loath to leave, for, in Plato's telling, accustomed to shadow, they fear the light. In Plato's hands, the formerly hallowed cave becomes the place where truth cannot be found, and where the soul cannot perceive the intelligible. It is where the idea of the Good cannot be attained, and where eternal darkness prevents men from the light of civilization, the bright orb of the sky god.

And so, whatever truth the sacred cave, womb of the Goddess, once held was banished by the light of Greek civilization. Only the Minotaur possessed the labyrinth. Only the prisoners remain in the once sacred cave.

Epilogue

Classical Greece represents an ending, but not, finally, *the* ending. Traces of the great Goddess remain in the goddesses of Rome, where they merged with goddesses from other traditions. Sacred imagery, such as the Goddess as divine nurse, the epiphanies of snake and pig, did not die off but continued, though sometimes robbed of symbolic meaning. Rites and rituals that had their beginnings in the sacred ceremonies of the Goddess continued throughout Roman times and then through the Judeo-Christian era as well. Farmers continued to offer first fruits to the earth, as their ancestors had before them. Once-sacred places and stones became, in folklore, places of magic and transformation. Women had, historically, long been in charge of birth, the preparation of the body for death, and the pharmacopoeia, and so it continued; bits and pieces of ancient rites that had originated with the worship of the Goddess were relayed from woman to woman. Language, in its etymological roots as well as its metaphors and expressions, retained the imprint of the old ways, and passed them on through the next generations. The sites of the Goddess retained their sacrality in local imagination and folklore, and thus first Greco-Roman temples and then churches were built on top of once sacred caves and ruins, and finally crucifixes adorned the ancient menhirs. The great Goddess' descendants were transformed locally as well, and went on as new personages and incarnations. But despite the underground life of what was, and is an incredible legacy, the Goddess and the human beings who shared her gender were confined behind locked doors in the house of the sky god. And until recently, only the patriarch held the keys.

The last words of *Sanctuaries of the Goddess* belong to a voice that tells us precisely what we must do to reclaim our past, the words of Muriel Rukeyser:

> MYTH
> Long afterward, Oedipus, old and blinded, walked the
> roads.   He smelled a familiar smell.   It was
> the Sphinx.   Oedipus said, "I want to ask one question.
> Why didn't I recognize my mother?"   "You gave the
> wrong answer," said the Sphinx.   "But that was what
> made everything possible," said Oedipus.   "No," she said.
> "When I asked, What walks on four legs in the morning,
> two at noon, and three in the evening, you answered,
> Man.   You didn't say anything about woman."
> "When you say Man," said Oedipus, "you include women
> too. Everyone knows that."   She said, "That's what
> you think."

Decorated Menhir, Brittany

Notes

1. Realms of the Goddess

1. See particularly Gertrude Rachel Levy's *Religious Conceptions of the Stone Age*, Vincent Scully's *The Earth, the Temple, and the Gods*, Marija Gimbutas' *The Language of the Goddess* and *The Civilization of the Goddess*, Sibylle von Cles-Reden's *The Realm of the Great Goddess*, Riane Eisler's *The Chalice and the Blade*, and Anne Baring and Jules Cashford's *The Myth of the Goddess*.
2. Scully, *The Earth*, 14
3. Gimbutas, *Language*, 321. Gimbutas, *Civilization*, 400.
4. Marinatos, *Minoan Sacrificial Ritual*, 14–15.
5. Meyer, *Ancient Mysteries*, 243.

2. The Sacred Cave

1. Levy, *Religious*, 9–13.
2. Ibid., 14.
3. Ibid., 14–15.
4. Ruspoli, *Cave of Lascaux*, 99.
5. Ibid., 101.
6. Windels, *Lascaux Cave Paintings*, 52.
7. Gimbutas, *Language*, 162–163.
8. Baring and Cashford, *Myth*, 7–8.
9. Gimbutas, *Language*, 51.
10. Ibid., 198.
11. Levy, *Religious*, 27.
12. Eliade, *A History*, 5–6.
13. Sandars, *Prehistoric Art*, 38.
14. Eliade, *A History*, 6.
15. James, *Prehistoric Religion*, 28–29.
16. Bataille, *Lascaux*, 20.
17. Leroi-Gourhan, *Treasures*, 305.
18. Gimbutas, *Language*, 304–306.
19. Raphael, *Prehistoric Cave Paintings*, 31
20. Marshack, *Roots*, 335, 336.
21. Sandars, *Prehistoric Art*, 70.
22. Delporte, *L'Image*, 64.
23. Ibid.
24. Ibid., 64. White, *Dark Caves*, 27.
25. Baring and Cashford, *Myth*, 21.
26. Marshack, *Roots*, 335–336.
27. Levy, *Religious*, 27.
28. Sandars, *Prehistoric Art*, 138.
29. Leroi-Gourhan, *Dawn of European*, 11.
30. Marshack, *Roots*, 173.
31. Eisler, *Chalice*, 6.

32. Ruspoli, *Cave of Lascaux*, 28.
33. Sandars, *Prehistoric Art*, 134.
34. Gimbutas, *Language*, 178. Campbell, *Primitive Mythology*, 300–304.
35. Baring and Cashford, *Myth*, 39.
36. Gimbutas, *Civilization*, 230.
37. Gimbutas, *Language*, 191.
38. Ibid., 258–260.
39. Johnson, *Lady*, 224.
40. Leroi-Gourhan, *Les Religions*, 137.
41. Gimbutas, *Language*, 175.

3. The Roots of Old Europe

1. Phillips, *Prehistory*, 148. The same point is made by Colin Renfrew in another context in *Emergence of Civilisation*, 265.
2. The dependence of this chapter on the work of Marija Gimbutas in interpreting the symbolic language of the Goddess cannot be overstated. I have limited notes to cases where the interpretation of a specific artifact is offered by Professor Gimbutas in one of her books. For a full explication of the symbols of the Goddess, please refer to the listing of Professor Gimbutas' works in the Bibliography.
3. Trump, *Central and Southern Italy*, 44–45.
4. Mellaart, *Çatal Hüyük*, 27.
5. Ibid., 177. Todd, *Çatal Hüyük in Perspective*, disputes that Hasan Dağ was the subject of the volcano painting and that it was the source of the settlement's obsidian, although without citing sources (47).
6. Mellaart, *Çatal Hüyük*, 176, 177.
7. Ibid., 135.
8. Ibid.
9. Gimbutas, *Civilization*, 255–256.
10. Mellaart, *Çatal Hüyük*, 207.
11. Gimbutas, *Civilization*, 256.
12. Mellaart, *Çatal Hüyük*, 164–165.
13. Ibid., 201–202.
14. Ibid., 165.
15. Gimbutas, Winn, and Shimabuku, *Achilleion*, 220.
16. Ibid., 213.
17. Srejović, *Europe's First*, 130.
18. Ibid.

19. Ibid., 82.
20. Ibid., 101.
21. Ibid., 118.
22. Ibid., 121.
23. Gimbutas, *Civilization*, 286.
24. Ibid., 64.
25. Tringham and Krstić, *Selevac*, 2.
26. Gimbutas, *Goddesses and Gods*, 61–65.
27. Chapman, *Vinča Culture*, 74.
28. Ibid.
29. Gimbutas, *Civilization*, 64.
30. Gimbutas, *Neolithic Macedonia*, 119.
31. Chapman, *Vinča Culture*, 73.
32. Gimbutas, *Goddesses and Gods*, 93.

4. The Flowering of the Goddess

1. Gimbutas, *Civilization*, 352ff.
2. Ibid., 292.
3. Brea, *Sicily*, 29.
4. Ibid., 52–53.
5. Gimbutas, *Language*, 178.
6. Brea, *Sicily*, 32. Sandars, *Prehistoric Art*, suggests a ritual of divine justice (150–154).
7. Gimbutas, *Language*, 178.
8. Brea, *Sicily*, 8.
9. Gimbutas, *Language*, 59–60.
10. Guido, *Sardinia*, 28–30.
11. Gimbutas, *Civilization*, 166.
12. Trump, "The Bonu Ighinu," 1–22.
13. Ibid., 6.
14. Trump, "Beyond Stratiography," 12–13.
15. Gimbutas, *Language*, 218–219.
16. Gimbutas, *Civilization*, 242–243.
17. Guido, *Sardinia*, 41–46.
18. Ibid., 51–56.
19. Ibid., 57.
20. Gimbutas, *Language*, 36.
21. Ibid., 78.
22. Gimbutas, *Civilization*, 170.
23. Guido, *Sardinia*, 59–61.
24. Gimbutas, *Civilization*, 290.
25. Renfrew, *Cycladic Spirit*, 31.
26. Ibid., 39.
27. Ibid., 39–41.
28. Renfrew, *Emergence of Civilisation*, 432.
29. Gimbutas, *Language*, 248.
30. Described in Renfrew, *Emergence of Civilisation*, 356–357.
31. Olaf Höckmann in Thimme, *Art and Culture*, 37ff.

32. Doumas, *Cycladic Culture*, 158.
33. Ibid., 99–100.
34. Renfrew, "Speculations," 24–31, for a summary of these arguments and Renfrew's own.
35. Ibid., 27–28. See also Renfrew, *Cycladic Spirit*, 99–101.
36. Doumas, *Cycladic Culture*, 94–95.
37. Renfrew, *Cycladic Spirit*, 165. Renfrew, *Emergence of Civilisation*, 419.

5. In and of the Earth: Malta

1. Von Cles-Reden, *Realm*, 80.
2. Zammit, *Prehistoric Malta*, 122.
3. Evans, J. D., *Malta*, 162.
4. Ibid., 71.
5. Von Cles-Reden, *Realm*, 71.
6. Levy, *Religious*, 13.
7. Zammit, *Prehistoric Malta*, 122–123.
8. J. D. Evans was the first to observe this connection. Evans, *Malta*, 89ff.
9. Trump, *Skorba*, 3–5. All descriptions of Skorba are drawn from this report of the excavation.
10. Evans, J. D., *Malta*, 91.
11. Ibid., 98. Gimbutas, *Civilization*, 176. Levy, *Religious*, 134.
12. Scully, *Earth*, 18–19.
13. Von Cles-Reden, *Realm*, 82.
14. Levy, *Religious*, 135.
15. Ibid., 136. Gimbutas, *Civilization*, 286.
16. Gimbutas, *Civilization*, 289.
17. Ibid., 262.
18. Zammit, *Prehistoric Malta*, 3–4.
19. Evans, J. D., *Malta*, 168.
20. Trump, *Prehistory*, 144.

6. Sacred Stones

1. Von Cles-Reden, *Realm*, 11.
2. Eliade, *History*, 117.
3. Burl, *Stone Circles*, 234.
4. Ibid., 312–313.
5. Burl, *Rites*, 38.
6. Burl, *Prehistoric Avebury*, 29, 66.
7. Clarke, Cowie, and Fox, *Symbols*, 79, 257.
8. Gimbutas, *Civilization*, 297.
9. Gimbutas, *Language*, 71.
10. Burl, *Rites*, 5.
11. Burl, *Prehistoric Avebury*, 95ff.
12. O'Riordan and Daniel, *New Grange*, 49. O'Kelly, *Newgrange*, 27, 33, 42, disagrees and questions

these points about the top, height, and whiteness.

13. Hock, R. E., "Some Henges and Hengiform Earthworks in Ireland," Ph.D. dissertation, University of Pennsylvania, 1975, cited in Burl, *Stone Circles*, 24.
14. Gimbutas, *Civilization*, 301.
15. Ibid.
16. O'Riordan, *New Grange*, 60–61. O'Kelly, *Newgrange*, 37. See O'Kelly on the roof box, 123ff.
17. O'Kelly, *Newgrange*, 126.
18. Eogan, *Excavations*, 11.
19. Eogan, *Knowth*, 66.
20. Ibid., 178, 183.
21. Gimbutas, *Civilization*, 304.
22. The descriptions of Stonehenge are drawn from Atkinson, *Stonehenge*, and Burl, *Stone Circles*.
23. The whole question of the purpose and orientation of Stonehenge has been vigorously and vociferously debated. See Wood, *Sun, Moon*, for an argument on Stonehenge as an observatory, and also Castelden, *Stonehenge People*. Meaden, *Goddess*, connects the meaning of the stone circles to meteorology unconvincingly. I have drawn my observations from Burl, *Stone Circles*, 305ff.
24. Gimbutas, *Goddesses and Gods*, 152.
25. Atkinson, *Stonehenge*, 169–170.
26. Burl, *Rites*, 109.
27. Atkinson, *Stonehenge*, 172ff.
28. Burl, *Rites*, 109.
29. Burl, *Stone Circles*, 314.
30. Burl, *Prehistoric Avebury*, 126–128. Dames, *Avebury Cycle*, offers a very close reading of the site in terms of puberty and other rites which hinges on a great deal of hypothetical reconstruction; see also Gadon, *Once and Future*, specifically the chapter entitled "Avebury: The Great Seasonal Drama of Her Life," which is based largely on Dames.
31. Burl, *Prehistoric Avebury*, 130.
32. Dames, *Silbury Treasure*, 66ff.
33. Burl, *Prehistoric Avebury*, 200ff. In his words, "Death and regeneration are the themes of Avebury."

7. The Goddess at the Peak: Crete

1. The indebtedness of this chapter to Vincent Scully's *The Earth, the Temple, and the Gods* cannot be overstated. Wherever possible, I have quoted Mr. Scully directly since he is, among other things, a wonderful writer.
2. Branigan, *Foundations*, 8–9.
3. See Hutchinson, *Prehistoric Crete*, 201ff., on the question of the actual location of the mythic caves.
4. Ibid., 202.
5. Hawkes, *Dawn*, 131.
6. Trump, *Prehistory*, 39–40.
7. Branigan, *Foundations*, 7.
8. Willetts, *Civilization*, 120.
9. Gimbutas, *Language*, 273.
10. Nilsson, *Minoan*, 223.
11. Hawkes, *Dawn*, 132.
12. James, *Prehistoric*, 64.
13. Rutowski, *Cult Places*, 53.
14. Levy, *Religious*, 214–215.
15. Gimbutas, *Language*, 151ff.
16. Branigan, *Foundations*, 84.
17. Gimbutas, *Language*, 312ff.
18. Johnson, *Lady*, 262. See also Gimbutas, *Language*, 316.
19. Levy, *Religious*, 214.
20. Branigan, *Foundations*, 107.
21. Platon, *Zakros*, 43.
22. Levy, *Religious*, 215.
23. Gimbutas, *Language*, 108.
24. Papaioannou, *Art*, 35.
25. Baring and Cashford, *Myth*, 112.
26. Levy, *Religious*, 214.
27. Scully, *Earth*, 11ff.
28. Platon, *Zakros*, 260.
29. Scully, *Earth*, 12–13.
30. Gimbutas, *Language*, 265ff.
31. Scully, *Earth*, 13.
32. Ibid.
33. Marinatos, *Minoan*, 6.
34. Nilsson, *Minoan*, 79–83.
35. Nilsson, *Minoan*, 135ff. Castleden, *Minoans*, 132.
36. See Renfrew, *Emergence*, 212–215. Hutchinson, *Prehistoric*, 102ff.
37. Levy, *Religious*, 235–236. Hawkes, *Dawn*, 143–146.
38. Harrison, *Epilegomena*, 179–181.
39. Platon, *Zakros*, 293.

8. Homer and the Goddess

1. Palmer, *Mycenaeans*, 121ff.
2. Gimbutas, *Language*, 318.
3. Scully, *Earth*, 38–40.
4. *Britannica*, 558.
5. Homer, *Iliad*, 391 (XVIII, 590ff.).
6. Nilsson, *Minoan*, 498–501.

7. For a different reading of this myth, see Gadon, *Once,* 105.
8. Taylor, "Obstacles," 95.
9. Nilsson, *Minoan,* 498–501.
10. Taylor, "Obstacles," 93–94.
11. Dimock, "Name," 60.
12. Homer, *Odyssey,* 94 (V, 234–236).
13. Harrison, *Prolegomena,* 284–285.

9. The Legacy of the Goddess: Greece

1. Mylonas, *Eleusis,* 23.
2. Connor, *Greek,* 31.
3. Cicero, 415 (*De Legibus,* II, XIV, 36).
4. Seneca, 293.
5. For the full text, see Meyer, *Ancient Mysteries.* Quotations in the text are from this edition.
6. Scully, *Earth,* 73.
7. Nilsson, *Minoan,* 520ff.
8. Kérenyi, *Eleusis,* 28–29. For a contemporary feminist vision of the Mysteries, see Keller, "The Eleusinian Mysteries."
9. Mylonas, *Eleusis,* 34ff.
10. Scully, *Earth,* 28–29.
11. Mylonas, *Eleusis,* 117.
12. Scully, *Earth,* 76.
13. This material is drawn from Mylonas, *Eleusis,* 247ff., which gives a detailed reconstruction of the Mysteries.
14. Scully, *Earth,* 74.
15. Ibid., 75.
16. Eliade, *Rites,* xiii.
17. Scully, *Earth,* 76.
18. Eliade, *Rites,* 110–111.
19. Cited in Meyer, *Ancient Mysteries,* 18–19.
20. Cited in Meyer, *Ancient Mysteries,* 19.
21. Mylonas, *Eleusis,* 273–274.
22. Evans, Arthur, *Palace of Minos,* 828–833.
23. Eliade, *History,* 271.
24. Aeschylus, *Oresteia,* 140.
25. Scully, *Earth,* 109.
26. Ibid.
27. See, however, Fontenrose, *Delphic,* 202–204, who disputes the "mania" of the priestess.
28. Harrison, *Themis,* 399.
29. Evans, Arthur, *Palace of Minos,* 840.
30. Eliade, *History,* 274.
31. Harrison, *Prolegomena,* 260–261.
32. Scully, *Earth,* 47ff.
33. Ibid., 57.
34. Ibid., 58.
35. Von Matt and Zanotti-Bianco, *Magna Graecia,* 46ff.
36. Ibid., 46.
37. Gimbutas, *Language,* 116–117.
38. Nilsson, *Minoan,* 503.
39. Scully, *Earth,* 80.
40. Baring and Cashford, *Myth,* 327.
41. Scully, *Earth,* 89.
42. Ibid.
43. Eliade, *History,* 282.
44. See Papaioannou, *Art,* for a reconstruction in photographs from various museum collections of the Parthenon sculptures, and also Robertson, *Parthenon.*
45. Eliade, *History,* 264.
46. Baring and Cashford, *Myth,* 338.
47. Snell, *Discovery,* 35.
48. Plato, *Dialogues,* 749.

Selected Bibliography

Aeschylus. *Oresteia.* Translated by Richmond Lattimore. Chicago and London: University of Chicago Press, 1953, 1973.

Atkinson, R. J. C. *Stonehenge.* New York: The Macmillan Company, 1956.

Barfield, Lawrence. *Northern Italy Before Rome.* New York and Washington: Praeger Publishers, 1972.

Baring, Anne, and Jules Cashford. *The Myth of the Goddess: Evolution of an Image.* London: Viking Arkana, 1991.

Bataille, Georges. *Lascaux or the Birth of Art.* Translated by Austyn Wainhouse. Lausanne: Skira Publishers, 1955.

Branigan, Keith. *The Foundations of Palatial Crete: A Survey of Crete in the Early Bronze Age.* New York: Praeger Publishers, 1970.

Brea, Bernabo L. *Sicily Before the Greeks.* New York: Frederick A. Praeger, 1957.

Burl, Aubrey. *Prehistoric Avebury.* New Haven, Conn., and London: Yale University Press, 1979.

————. *Rites of the Gods.* London: J. M. Dent & Sons, 1981.

————. *The Stone Circles of the British Isles.* New Haven, Conn., and London: Yale University Press, 1976.

Campbell, Joseph. *Primitive Mythology: The Masks of God.* New York: Penguin Books, 1987.

Castelden, Rodney. *Minoans: Life in the Bronze Age.* London: Routledge, 1990.

————. *The Stonehenge People: An Exploration of Life in Neolithic Britain.* London and New York: Routledge, 1987.

Chapman, John. *The Vinča Culture of South-East Europe.* Oxford: BAR International Series, 117 (1), 1981.

Childe, V. Gordon. *The Dawn of Civilization.* New York: Alfred A. Knopf, 1958.

Cicero. *De Re Publica, De Legibus.* Translated by Clinton Walker Keyes. Cambridge: Harvard University Press, 1966.

Clarke, D. V., T. G. Cowie, and Andrew Fox. *Symbols of Power at the Time of Stonehenge.* Edinburgh: National Museum of Antiquities, 1985.

von Cles-Reden, Sibylle. *The Realm of the Great Goddess: The Story of the Megalith Builders.*

Translated by Eric Mosbacher. Englewood Cliffs, N.J.: Prentice-Hall, 1962.

Connor, E. Robert, ed. *Greek Orations: Lysias, Isocrates, Demosthenes, Aeschines, Hyperides, and the Letter of Philip.* Ann Arbor: University of Michigan Press, 1966.

Crawford, O. G. S. *The Eye Goddess.* New York: The Macmillan Company, n.d.

Dames, Michael. *The Avebury Cycle.* London: Thames & Hudson, 1977.

————. *The Silbury Treasure: The Great Goddess Rediscovered.* London: Thames & Hudson, 1976.

Delporte, Henri. *L'Image de la Femme dans l'art préhistorique.* Paris: A. et J. Picard, 1979.

Dimock, George E., Jr. "The Name of Odysseus," in *Essays on the Odyssey.* Edited by Charles H. Taylor, Jr. Bloomington and London: Indiana University Press, 1963.

Doumas, Christos. *Cycladic Art: Ancient Sculpture and Pottery from the N. P. Goulandris Collection.* London: British Museum Publications, 1983.

————. *Cycladic Culture: Naxos in the Third Millennium B.C.* Athens: N. P. Goulandris Foundation — Museum of Cycladic Art, 1990.

Eisler, Riane. *The Chalice and the Blade: Our History, Our Future.* San Francisco: HarperCollins, 1987.

Eliade, Mircea. *A History of Religious Ideas,* vol. I. Translated by Willard R. Trask. Chicago: University of Chicago Press, 1978.

————. *Rites and Symbols of Initiation: The Mysteries of Birth and Rebirth.* Translated by Willard R. Trask. New York: Harper Torchbooks, 1958.

Encyclopaedia Britannica, 11th edition (1911).

Eogan, George. *Excavations at Knowth: Smaller Passage Tombs, Neolithic Occupation and Beaker Activity.* Dublin: Royal Irish Academy, 1984.

————. *Knowth and the Passage Tombs of Ireland.* London: Thames & Hudson, 1986.

Evans, Sir Arthur. *The Palace of Minos,* vol. II, part II. London: Macmillan and Company, 1928.

Evans, J. D. *Malta.* New York: Frederick A. Praeger, 1959.

Fontenrose, Joseph. *The Delphic Oracle.* Berkeley and Los Angeles: University of California Press, 1978.

Gadon, Elinor W. *The Once and Future Goddess.* San Francisco: Harper & Row, 1989.

Gelard, Richard G. *The Traveler's Key to Ancient Greece: A Guide to the Sacred Places of Ancient Greece.* New York: Alfred A. Knopf, 1989.

Gimbutas, Marija. *The Civilization of the Goddess.* San Francisco: Harper San Francisco, 1991.

———. *The Goddesses and Gods of Old Europe: Myths and Cult Images.* Berkeley and Los Angeles: University of California Press, 1982.

———. *The Language of the Goddess.* San Francisco: Harper & Row, 1989.

———. *Neolithic Macedonia.* Monumenta Archaeologica, vol. I. Los Angeles: The Archaeological Institute, 1976.

Gimbutas, Marija, Shann Winn, and Daniel Shimabuku. *Achilleion: A Neolithic Settlement in Thessaly, Greece, 6400–5600.* Los Angeles: University of California at Los Angeles, 1989.

Göttner-Abendroth, Heide. *The Dancing Goddess: Principles of a Matriarchal Aesthetic.* Translated by Maureen T. Krause. Boston: Beacon Press, 1991.

Graves, Robert. *The Greek Myths,* 2 vols., revised edition. London: Penguin Books, 1960.

Grinsell, Leslie V. *Burrow, Pyramid and Tomb: Ancient Burial Customs in Egypt, the Mediterranean, and the British Isles.* London: Thames & Hudson, 1975.

Guido, Margaret. *Sardinia.* New York: Frederick A. Praeger, 1964.

Harrison, Jane Ellen. *Epilegomena to the Study of Greek Religion and Themis.* New Hyde Park, N.Y.: University Books, 1962.

———. *Prolegomena to the Study of Greek Religion.* Cleveland and New York: World Publishing Company, 1959.

———. *Themis: A Study in the Social Origins of Greek Religion.* Cleveland and New York: World Publishing Company, 1962.

Harvey, Paul. *The Oxford Companion to Classical Literature.* Oxford: Oxford University Press, 1946.

Hawkes, Jacquetta. *Dawn of the Gods.* London: Chatto & Windus, 1968.

Homer. *The Iliad.* Translated by Richmond Lattimore. Chicago and London: University of Chicago Press, 1951.

———. *The Odyssey of Homer.* Translated by Richmond Lattimore. New York: Harper & Row, 1968.

Hood, Sinclair. *The Arts in Prehistoric Greece.* London: Penguin Books, 1978.

Hutchinson, R. W. *Prehistoric Crete.* Baltimore: Penguin Books, 1962.

James, E. O. *The Cult of the Mother Goddess.* London: Thames & Hudson, 1959.

———. *From Cave to Cathedral.* New York: Frederick A. Praeger, 1965.

———. *Prehistoric Religion: A Study in Prehistoric Archaeology.* New York: Barnes & Noble, 1962.

Johnson, Buffie. *Lady of the Beasts: Ancient Images of the Goddess and Her Animals.* San Francisco: Harper & Row, 1988.

Keller, Mara Lynn. "The Eleusinian Mysteries of Demeter and Persephone: Fertility, Sexuality, and Rebirth," *Journal of Feminist Studies in Religion.* Spring 1988, vol. 4, 1.

Kérenyi, C. *Eleusis: Archetypal Image of Mother and Daughter.* Translated by Ralph Mannheim. New York: Schocken Books, 1977.

Knox, Bernard. *Oedipus at Thebes: Sophocles' Tragic Hero and His Time.* New York: W. W. Norton, 1971.

Lerner, Gerda. *The Creation of Patriarchy.* New York and Oxford: Oxford University Press, 1986.

Leroi-Gourhan, André. *The Dawn of European Art: An Introduction to Paleolithic Cave Painting.* Translated by Sara Champion. London and New York: Cambridge University Press, 1982.

———. *Les Religions de la Préhistoire.* Paris: Presses universitaires de France, 1964.

———. *Treasures of Prehistoric Art.* Translated by Norbert Guterman. New York: Harry N. Abrams, n.d.

Levy, Gertrude Rachel. *Religious Conceptions of the Stone Age.* New York: Harper & Row, 1963.

Marinatos, Nanno. *Minoan Sacrificial Ritual: Culture, Practice, and Ritual.* Stockholm: Swedish Institute, 1986.

Maringer, Johannes, and Hans-Georgi Bandi. *Art in the Ice Age.* New York: Frederick A. Praeger, 1953.

Marshack, Alexander. *The Roots of Civilization.* Mount Kisco, N.Y.: Moyer Bell Ltd., 1990.

von Matt, Leonard, and Umberto Zanotti-Bianco. *Magna Graecia.* Translated by Herbert Hoffman. New York: Universe Books, 1962.

Meaden, George T. *The Goddess of the Stones.* London: Souvenir Press, 1991.

Mellaart, James. *The Archaeology of Ancient Turkey.* Totowa, N.J.: Rowan and Littlefield, 1978.

———. *Çatal Hüyük: A Neolithic Town in Anatolia.* New York: McGraw-Hill Book Company, 1967.

Meyer, Marvin E., ed. *The Ancient Mysteries: A Sourcebook.* San Francisco: Harper & Row, 1987.

Mylonas, George E. *Eleusis and the Eleusinian Mysteries.* Princeton, N.J.: Princeton University Press, 1961.

Neumann, Erich. *The Great Mother: An Analysis of the Archetype.* Translated by Ralph Mannheim. Bollingen series XLVII. Princeton, N.J.: Princeton University Press, 1974.

Nilsson, Martin P. *The Minoan-Mycenaean Religion and Its Survival in Greek Religion.* Lund, Sweden: C. W. K. Gleerup, 1950.

O'Kelly, Michael J. *Newgrange: Archaeology, Art and Legend.* London: Thames & Hudson, 1982.

O'Riordan, Sean P., and Glyn Daniel. *New Grange and the Bend of the Boyne.* New York: Frederick A. Praeger, 1964.

Palmer, Leonard R. *Mycenaeans and Minoans: Aegean Prehistory in Light of the Linear B Tablets.* New York: Alfred A. Knopf, 1962.

Papaioannou, Kostas. *The Art of Greece.* Translated by I. Mark Paris. New York: Harry N. Abrams, 1989.

Papathanassopoulos, G. *Neolithic and Cycladic Civilization.* Athens: Mellisa Publishing House, 1981.

Pendlebury, J. D. S. *The Archaeology of Crete.* London: Methuen, 1939; reprint 1965.

Phillips, Patricia. *The Prehistory of Europe.* Bloomington: Indiana University Press, 1980.

Plato. *The Collected Dialogues.* Edited by Edith Hamilton and Huntington Cairns. Bollingen series LXXI. Princeton, N.J.: Princeton University Press, 1963.

Platon, Nicholas. *Zakros: The Discovery of a Lost Palace of Ancient Crete.* New York: Charles Scribner's Sons, 1971.

Raphael, Max. *Prehistoric Cave Paintings.* Translated by Norbert Guterman. New York: Pantheon Books, 1945.

Renfrew, Colin, ed. *British Prehistory: A New Outline.* Park Ridge, N.J.: Noyes Press, 1974.

———. *The Cycladic Spirit: Masterpieces from the Nicholas P. Goulandris Collection.* New York: Harry N. Abrams, 1991.

———. *The Emergence of Civilisation: The Cyclades and the Aegean in the Third Millennium B.C.* London: Methuen & Co., 1972.

———. "Speculations on the Use of Early Cycladic Sculpture," in *Cycladic Studies in Memory of N. P. Goulandris.* Edited by J. Lesley Fitton. London: British Museum Publications, 1984.

Richter, Gisela M. *A Handbook of Greek Art.* London and New York: Phaidon, 1959.

Robertson, Martin. *The Parthenon Frieze.* New York: Oxford University Press, 1975.

Ruspoli, Mario. *The Cave of Lascaux: The Final Photographs.* New York: Harry N. Abrams, 1987.

Rutowski, Bogdan. *The Cult Places of the Aegean.* New Haven, Conn.: Yale University Press, 1986.

Sandars, N. K. *Prehistoric Art.* London: Penguin Books, 1985.

Scully, Vincent. *The Earth, the Temple, and the Gods.* New York: Frederick A. Praeger, 1969.

Seneca. *Naturales Quaestiones,* vol. II. Translated by Thomas H. Corcoran. Cambridge: Harvard University Press, 1972.

Snell, Bruno. *The Discovery of the Mind: Origins of European Thought.* Translated by T. G. Rosenmeyer. New York and Evanston, Ill.: Harper Torchbooks, 1960.

Srejović, Dragoslav. *Europe's First Monumental Sculpture: New Discoveries at Lepenski Vir.* New York: Stein & Day Publishers, 1972.

Stone, Merlin. *When God Was a Woman.* New York: Harcourt Brace Jovanovich, 1976.

Taylor, Charles H., Jr. "The Obstacles to Odysseus' Return," in *Essays On the Odyssey.* Edited by Charles H. Taylor, Jr. Bloomington and London: Indiana University Press, 1963.

Thimme, Jürgen, ed. *Art and Culture of the Cyclades in the Third Millennium B.C.* Translated and edited by Pat Getz-Preziozi. Chicago and London: University of Chicago Press, 1977.

Todd, Ian A. *Çatal Hüyük in Perspective.* Menlo Park, Calif.: Cummings Publishing Company, 1976.

Torbrugge, Water. *Prehistoric European Art.* New York: Harry N. Abrams, 1968.

Tringham, Ruth, and Dusan Krstić. *Selevac: A Neolithic Town in Yugoslavia.* Monumenta Archaeologica, vol. 15. Los Angeles: UCLA/The Institute of Archaeology, 1990.

Trump, D. H. "Beyond Stratiography — The Bonu Ighinu Project," in *Studies in Sardinian Archaeology,* vol. 2. Edited by Miriam S. Balmuth. Ann Arbor: University of Michigan Press, 1968.

———. "The Bonu Ighinu Project and the Sardinian Neolithic," in *Studies in Sardinian Archaeology.* Edited by Miriam S. Balmuth and Robert J. Rowland, Jr. Ann Arbor: University of Michigan Press, 1984.

———. *Central and Southern Italy Before Rome.* London: Thames & Hudson, 1966.

———. *The Prehistory of the Mediterranean.* New Haven, Conn.: Yale University Press, 1980.

———. *Skorba.* Oxford: The Society of Antiquaries, 1966.

Walker, Barbara G. *The Woman's Encyclopedia of Myths and Secrets.* San Francisco: Harper & Row, 1983.

Wasson, R. Gordon, Carl A. P. Ruck, and Albert Hoffman. *The Road to Eleusis.* New York: Harcourt Brace Jovanovich, 1978.

White, R. *Dark Caves, Bright Visions: Life in Ice Age Europe.* New York: W. W. Norton and Company/American Museum of Natural History, 1986.

Willetts, R. F. *The Civilization of Ancient Crete.* London: B. T. Batsford, 1977.

Windels, Fernand. *The Lascaux Cave Paintings.* New York: The Viking Press, 1950.

Wood, John Edwin. *Sun, Moon, and Standing Circles.* Oxford: Oxford University Press, 1970.

Zammit, Themistocles. *The Hal-Saflieni Hypogeum.* Malta: 1926.

———. *Prehistoric Malta: The Tarxien Temples.* Oxford: Oxford University Press, 1930.

Acknowledgments

Since I am trained in literature and neither a professional archaeologist nor an art historian, this book could not have been written without the scholars and their scholarship on which I have relied. While the footnotes and bibliography reveal all, I would like to thank — alas, without having studied with either of them, but having the benefit and privilege of their publications — Professors Marija Gimbutas and Vincent Scully. This book would not have been written without my editor, Lindley Boegehold: her initial suggestions and continued support made it happen. The book would not have been completed without the endless patience and support of Peter and Alexandra. The fine training I received as an undergraduate and graduate student permitted me to go back to working in research libraries after a twenty-year hiatus, for which I thank principally Professors Robert Bamberg, Joel Connaroe, Edward Tayler, and Jacob Smit, and the late William York Tindall, all of whom taught me to read hard, despite the darkness of the stacks.

Genuine gratitude to all who helped with the nightmare of picture research, and to those whose work has been reproduced, with permission, listed on page 212. To wit: the British Tourist Authority; the Rowland Company and the Greek National Tourist Organization and their photographer Meredith Pillon; the Irish Tourist Board; the French Tourist Agency; the Tourist Office of Spain; the Turkish Cultural and Information Office; Liberty Eco of the Greek Press and Information Agency, who got me through the labyrinth of Crete and found me the Ministry of Culture and its pictures; the Italian Cultural Institute; the Austrian Institute; the British Museum; The Travel Image; and the absolutely terrific people at Art Resource, where the range of the files is matched by the goodwill of the folks. I especially thank the photographers, credited elsewhere, who shared their work and interest: Blaine Harrington III; Cindy A. Pavlinac of Sacred Land Photography, a friend found; Michael Reagan; and Robert (Bob) Zehring, the intrepid photographer of Malta and elsewhere, who was, among other things, very nice.

Thanks to Claudia Karabaic Sargent, a partner in other ventures, who once again lent me her talent and love. A special award to Lori Stein for her deeds of fax, goodness, and Goddess. And a thanks to Erika, for finding the book when I couldn't.

Picture Credits

PAGE 2. Goddess and Child. Erich Lessing/Art Resource, New York.

PAGE 8. Temple of Athena—Paestum. Copyright © 1994 Robert Zehring.

PAGE 10. Standing Stones of Callanish. Courtesy of the British Tourist Authority.

PAGE 12. Autumn Dawn over Crete. Copyright © 1994 Cindy A. Pavlinac.

PAGE 14. Spiral at New Grange. Courtesy of the Irish Tourist Board.

PAGE 15. Lascaux Bull. Courtesy of the French Government Tourist Office.

PAGE 17. Cistern at Zakros. Copyright © 1994 Cindy A. Pavlinac.

PAGE 18. New Grange. Courtesy of the Irish Tourist Board.

PAGE 20. Locmariaquer, Brittany. Copyright © 1994 Cindy A. Pavlinac.

PAGE 21. Owl Goddess. Giraudon/Art Resource, New York.

PAGE 22. Snake Goddess. Courtesy of the Greek Ministry of Culture; Mother Goddess. Courtesy of the Greek Ministry of Culture.

PAGE 23. Cretan Shell. Copyright © 1994 Cindy A. Pavlinac.

PAGE 24. Lascaux: The Rotunda. Courtesy of the French Government Tourist Office.

PAGE 27. Willendorf Goddess. Courtesy of the Austrian Institute; Detail of Wall Art from Pech-Merle. Courtesy of the French Government Tourist Office.

PAGE 28. Grimaldi Goddess. Erich Lessing/Art Resource, New York; Lespugue Goddess. Scala/Art Resource, New York; Goddess of Sireuil. Giraudon/Art Resource, New York.

PAGE 33. Laussel Goddess. Scala/Art Resource, New York.

PAGE 36. Detail from the Frieze of the Rotunda, Lascaux. Courtesy of the French Government Tourist Office.

PAGE 37. Lascaux. Courtesy of the French Government Tourist Office.

PAGE 38. Lascaux. Courtesy of the French Government Tourist Office.

PAGE 40. Altamira. Courtesy of the Tourist Office of Spain.

PAGE 43. Lascaux. Courtesy of the French Government Tourist Office.

PAGE 44. Enthroned Goddess. Erich Lessing/Art Resource, New York.

PAGE 47. Çatal Hüyük. Courtesy of the Turkish Cultural and Information Office.

PAGE 52. Hamangia Goddess. Erich Lessing/Art Resource, New York; Goddess from Tell Azmak. Erich Lessing/Art Resource, New York.

PAGE 53. Stiff Nudes. Erich Lessing/Art Resource, New York.

PAGE 56. Lepenski Vir Goddess. Erich Lessing/Art Resource, New York; Lepenski Vir Goddess. Giraudon/Art Resource, New York.

PAGE 58. Ritual Objects. Erich Lessing/Art Resource, New York.

PAGE 61. Goddess and Child. Erich Lessing/Art Resource, New York; Temple Model. Giraudon/Art Resource, New York.

PAGE 62. Seated Goddess. Erich Lessing/Art Resource, New York; Altar Table. Erich Lessing/Art Resource, New York.

PAGE 63. Bird Goddess. Erich Lessing/Art Resource, New York.

PAGE 64. Island of Thera. Copyright © 1994 Robert Zehring.

PAGE 67. Rock-Cut Tomb at Agrigento. Copyright © 1994 Robert Zehring.

PAGE 70. Tomb at S. Andrea Priu. Copyright © 1994 Claudia Karabaic Sargent, after a drawing in Guido, *Sardinia*.

PAGE 71. Tomb at Bonorva. Copyright © 1994 The Travel Image.

PAGE 72. Sernobi Goddess. Scala/Art Resource, New York.

PAGE 74. Delos. Copyright © 1994 Cindy A. Pavlinac.

PAGE 79. Cycladic Goddess. Art Resource, New York; Cycladic Goddess. Erich Lessing/Art Resource, New York.

PAGE 80. Cycladic Harpist. Copyright © 1994 Cindy A. Pavlinac.

PAGE 82. Ġgantija Temple. Copyright © 1994 Robert Zehring.

PAGE 87. Ghar Dalam Cave. Copyright © 1994 Robert Zehring.

PAGE 88. Ġgantija Temple. Copyright © 1994 Robert Zehring.

Index

Designed by Martine Bruel
Text set in Palatino, Palatino Italic and Bold by Hamilton Phototype
Titles in Busorama Light and Medium by Composing Room of New England
Printed and bound by Tien Wah Press Ltd., Singapore